P9-DET-921

# THE SIZE OF THE SOUL

# *The Size of the Soul*

## A.W. Tozer

## Compiled by Harry Verploegh

CHRISTIAN PUBLICATIONS
CAMP HILL, PENNSYLVANIA

Christian Publications
3825 Hartzdale Drive, Camp Hill, PA 17011

*The mark of* ✝ *vibrant faith*

ISBN: 0-87509-497-X
LOC Catalog Card Number: 92-73704
© 1992 by Christian Publications
All rights reserved
Printed in the United States of America

94 95 96  5  4  3  2

Cover Photo: Patricia Sgrignoli, Positive Images

# CONTENTS

*Foreword* 1

1  *The Size of the Soul* 5

2  *What About Revival?—Part I* 8

3  *What About Revival?—Part II* 12

4  *What About Revival?—Part III* 17

5  *What About Revival?—Part IV* 22

6  *The Use and Abuse of Good Books—Part I* 27

7  *The Use and Abuse of Good Books—Part II* 31

8  *The Use and Abuse of Good Books—Part III* 36

9  *The Use and Abuse of Good Books—Part IV* 41

10  *The Use and Abuse of Good Books—Part V* 46

11  *Who Does the Work of God?* 51

12  *Not Too Many But the Wrong Kind* 54

13  *Words without Meaning Are Idle Words* 59

14  *A Needed Reformation* 64

15  *Perpetual Sacrifice or Perpetual Efficacy?* 68

16  *The Corrosive Effects of a Fretful Spirit* 70

17  *No Sin Is Private* 74

18  *Zeal: What Does It Prove?* 78

19  *Religion: No Substitute for Action* 83

20  *Hope: The Universal Treasure—Part I* 88

21  *Hope: The Universal Treasure—Part II* 92

22  *The Church Wins a Pyrrhic Victory* 96

96248

23  Let No One Rob You  101
of Your Christian Confidence

24  The Causes of Religious Confusion  106
—Part I

25  The Causes of Religious Confusion  111
—Part II

26  The Problem of Numbers  115

27  Not Papal Infallibility, But the Witness  120

28  The Gifts of Prophetic Insight  125
Imperative Today—Part I

29  The Gifts of Prophetic Insight  130
Imperative Today—Part II

30  Optimist or Pessimist?  135

31  We Are All Heretics by Nature  140

32  The Shadow of Consequences  145

33  It Is Essential That We Think Like God  149

34  The New Birth Is a Mystery  152

35  Christian—Or Only a Student  157
Christian?

36  A Word About Superstition  162

37  More About Superstition  166

38  Thankful? Yes, But to Whom?  171

39  Not Peace, But a Sword  175

40  Root out of a Dry Ground  179

41  Strength from the Indwelling Spirit  183

42  Divine Love Is Neither Blind Nor Dumb  187

43  What Easter Is About  192

# Foreword

This book is the 12th in a series containing editorials written by A.W. Tozer while he was editor of *Alliance Life* (formerly *The Alliance Witness*) from 1950 to 1963.

In 1794 Joseph Joubert said, "Big words claim too much attention." There are no big words here. It is remarkable how clearly and succinctly Tozer expressed himself so that no one, though a fool, need miss his meaning. He appeals wonderfully to the average as well as the erudite mind among us. ". . . in his pen, language was a lively instrument . . . ever accompanied with the gift of wisdom and spiritual discernment." Is it possible that this wisdom and discernment were the result of the following experience? Tozer wrote:

> I was 19 years old, earnestly in prayer, kneeling in the front room of my mother-

in-law's home, when I was baptized with a mighty infusion of the Holy Ghost . . . I know with assurance what God did for me and within me and that nothing on the outside held any important meaning. In desperation, and in faith, I took that leap away from everything that was unimportant to that which was most important—to be possessed by the Spirit of the Living God!

Any tiny work that God has ever done through me and through my ministry for Him dates back to that hour when I was filled with the Spirit. That is why I plead for the spiritual life of the Body of Christ and the eternal ministries of the Eternal Spirit through God's children—His instruments.

Was Tozer's baptism of the Holy Spirit (an experience not talked about much these days) the secret of his communicating power? The Scripture says, "Be filled with the Spirit" (Ephesians 5:18). Hopefully A.W. Tozer will, with these words, help us to recover the "spiritual life of the Body of Christ."

In addition to this new collection of editorials, a wealth of Tozer words can be found in the previous books in this series:

1955  *The Root of the Righteous*
1959  *Born After Midnight*

1960 *Of God and Men*
1964 *That Incredible Christian*
1966 *Man: The Dwelling Place of God*
1970 *God Tells the Man Who Cares*
1986 *The Set of the Sail*
1987 *The Next Chapter After the Last*
1988 *We Travel an Appointed Way*
1989 *This World: Playground or Battleground?*
1991 *The Price of Neglect*
1992 *The Size of the Soul*
1993 *The Warfare of the Spirit*

# The Size of the Soul

Persons out of Christ often try to comfort themselves with the remembrance that they have never in their lives committed any really great sin. Little trifling acts of wrongdoing perhaps, but nothing of any consequence, so surely God will overlook their rather insignificant transgressions when He settles their accounts.

In the first place, a man's status before God is decided not by the number and enormity of his sins but by whether those sins have or have not been forgiven, whether he is on God's side or the side of the devil.

The soldier who mutinies is held responsible for his mutiny even if he does nothing more than stand up and let himself be counted among the rebels. His crime lies in his break with his superiors and his willingness to go along with the enemies of his country. That he performs no extraordinary feats of violence may mean no more than that he is an ordinary fellow incapable of great deeds of any sort for or against his country.

Sins of great magnitude may indicate an energy of soul which if turned in a right direction can lead far up the way toward spiritual perfection. Conversely, there is a meanness of soul that inhibits and restricts the scope and intensity of even the most common activities. When such a soul is converted, it may be only to mediocrity.

On his own testimony Paul before his conversion was a great sinner (1 Timothy 1:15). He persecuted Christians with great violence and wrought havoc with the followers of Christ. After his spectacular about-face he turned his magnificent equipment over to the Lord and the whole world knows the result. The same energy of soul that had made him a dangerous enemy of the Christian faith made him a powerful advocate of that faith once his eyes had been opened.

From this we may learn that feebleness and timidity are not to be confused with righteousness. To sin but weakly is not the same as to do good. Lack of moral energy may prevent a man from enjoying himself in sin, but he is in sin nevertheless. His weak effort at neutrality does not deceive God who knows the secrets of every man's heart.

The size of a man's soul is likely to determine

his success or failure in the rough, competitive world of the 20th century. And after his conversion to Christ, it will go far to determine his usefulness in the kingdom of God. Undoubtedly there are many genuine Christians who are not doing much for their fellow men nor for the Church into which they were born by the miracle of the Spirit's regeneration. Such as these need to hear the words of Christ, "You will receive power when the Holy Spirit comes on you" (Acts 1:8). The only hope for a restricted heart is the mighty inworking of the Spirit. He can enlarge the mansion of the soul; but only He can do it.

# What About
# Revival?—Part I

*This Could Be the Year Revival Comes*

There seems to be a notion abroad that if we talk enough and pray enough, revival will set in like a stock market boom or a winning streak on a baseball club. We appear to be waiting for some sweet chariot to swing low and carry us into the Big Rock Candy Mountain of religious experience.

Well, it is a pretty good rule that if everyone is saying something it is not likely to be true; or, if it has truth at the bottom, it has been so distorted by wrong emphasis as to have the effect of error in its practical outworking. And such, I believe, is much of the revival talk we hear today.

My reason for doubt of the soundness of it is that we appear to conceive of revival as a kind of benign miracle, a feverish renaissance of religious activity which will come upon us, leaving us morally just as we are now, except that we will be a lot happier and there will be a great many more of us. It's a good talking point and it has an aura of superior godliness about it; but the trouble is that it is just not true.

Our mistake is that we want God to send revival on our terms. We want to get the power of God into our hands, to call it to us that it may work for us in promoting and furthering our kind of Christianity. We want still to be in charge, guiding the chariot through the religious sky in the direction we want it to go, shouting "Glory to God," it is true, but modestly accepting a share of the glory for ourselves in a nice inoffensive sort of way. We are calling on God to send fire on our altars, completely ignoring the fact that they are *our* altars and not God's. And like the prophets of Baal we are working ourselves into a frenzy as if we could by violence command the arm of the Almighty.

The whole error results from a confused notion of revival and a failure to recognize the moral laws that underlie the kingdom of God. God never moves whimsically; His ways are never impulsive or erratic. He never sends judgment unless there has been a violation of His laws, nor does He send blessing apart from obedience to those laws. So precise are His movements both in justice and in mercy that an intelligent observer, aware of the circumstances, could predict with complete accuracy any visitation of judgment or grace God might send to a nation, a church or an individual.

Of this we may be certain: We cannot continue to ignore God's will as expressed in the Scriptures and expect to secure the aid of God's Spirit. God has given us a complete blueprint for the Church and He requires that we adhere to it 100 percent. Message, morals and methods are there, and we are under strict obligation to be faithful to all three. Today we have the strange phenomenon of a company of Christians solemnly protesting to heaven and earth the purity of their Bible creed, and at the same time following the unregenerate world in their methods and managing only with difficulty to keep their moral standards from sinking out of sight. Coldness, worldliness, pride, boasting, lying, misrepresenting, love of money, exhibitionism—all these things are practiced by professedly orthodox Christians, not in secret but in plain sight and often as a necessary part of the whole religious show.

It will take more than talk and prayer to bring revival. There must be a return to the Lord *in practice* before our prayers will be heard in heaven. We dare not continue to trouble God's way if we want Him to bless ours. Joshua sent his army up to conquer Ai, only to see them hurled back with bloody losses. He threw himself to the ground on his face before the Ark and complained to the Lord.

> The LORD said to Joshua, "Stand up! What are you doing down on your face? Israel has sinned; they have violated my covenant . . . That is why the Israelites cannot stand against their enemies . . . because they have been made liable to destruction. I will not be with you anymore unless you destroy whatever among you is devoted to destruction." (Joshua 7:10–12)

If we are foolish enough to do it, we may spend the new year vainly begging God to send revival, while we blindly overlook His requirements and continue to break His laws. Or we can begin now to obey and learn the blessedness of obedience. The Word of God is before us. We have only to read and do what is written there and revival is assured. It will come as naturally as the harvest comes after the plowing and the planting.

Yes, this could be the year the revival comes. It's strictly up to us.

# CHAPTER 3

# What About
# Revival?—Part II

*Personal Revival*

Revival may be experienced on three levels,
viz., in the individual, the church or the
community.

It is impossible to have a community revival
where there has not been a church revival, and
unless at least a few individuals seek and obtain
a spiritual transformation in their own hearts,
there can be no hope for their church, for a
church is composed of individual Christians.

It is a mere commonplace to sing or pray,
"Lord, send a revival, and let it begin in me."
Where else can a spiritual quickening take
place but in the individual life? There is no
abstract "church" which can be revivified apart

from the men and women who compose it. The vague notion that there is somewhere a mysterious Body of Christ whose members are unknown, an invisible company upon whom the Holy Spirit can fall in answer to prayer, is a grand fallacy. It serves as a hiding place from reality to believe that such an unidentified superchurch actually exists apart from the plain ordinary people we see in our Christian gatherings and in our churches from week to week. But we may as well face the truth: Christians are people and people can be identified. They have names and faces and homes and friends and jobs. They keep house, go to school, drive trucks, buy, sell, travel, eat and bathe and sleep exactly as other people do. The seed of God is in them and their names are written in heaven, but they are not invisible. The world knows who the Christians are.

That "glorious band, the chosen few, on whom the Spirit came" at Pentecost, were not wraiths nor were they composed of an extract of pure humanity dwelling on another plane. They were people. The names of some of them are listed by the Holy Spirit. Though it did not suit God's purpose to furnish us with a complete roster of every one present, those mentioned were certainly human enough. When the Spirit came on that memorable day He could only fall upon persons who were present, who could be identified, who were known to each other and to the community.

There was no invisible body for Him to enter. He entered the bodies and souls of the men and women who were in that prayer meeting.

No church is any better or worse than the individual Christians who compose it. To look beyond the known members to some mysterious group which is imagined to be there, secretly prepared for a revival, is to err seriously in a province where error can be costly.

One consequence of our failure to see clearly the true nature of revival is that we wait for years for some supernatural manifestation that never comes, overlooking completely our own individual place in the desired awakening. Whatever God may do for a church must be done in the single unit, the one certain man or woman. Some things can happen only to the isolated, single person; they cannot be experienced en masse. Statistics show, for instance, that 100 babies are born in a certain city on a given day. Yet the birth of each baby is for that baby a unique experience, an isolated, personal thing. Fifty people die in a plane crash; while they die together they die separately, one at a time, each one undergoing the act of death in a loneliness of soul as utter as if he alone had died. Both birth and death are experienced by the individual in a loneness as complete as if only that one person had ever known them.

Three thousand persons were converted at Pentecost, but each one met his sin and his Savior alone. The spiritual birth, like the natural one, is for each one a unique, separate experience shared in by no one. And so with that uprush of resurgent life we call revival. It can come to the individual only. Though a visitation of divine life reaches 75 persons at once (as among the Moravian Brethren at Dusseldorf), yet it comes to each one singly. There can exist no collective body of believers that can be revived apart from the units that compose the body.

Understood aright these are truths full of great encouragement and good hope. Nothing can hinder you or me from experiencing the revival we need. It is a matter for God and the solitary heart. Nothing can prevent the spiritual rejuvenation of the soul that insists upon having it. Though that solitary man must live and walk among persons religiously dead, he may experience the great transformation as certainly and as quickly as if he were in the most spiritual church in the world.

The man that *will* have God's best becomes at once the object of the personal attention of the Holy Spirit. Such a man will not be required to wait for the rest of the church to come alive. He will not be penalized for the failures of his fellow Christians, nor be asked to forego the blessing till his sleepy brethren catch up. God deals with the individual heart as exclusively as if only one existed.

If this should seem to be an unduly individualistic approach to revival, let it be remembered that religion is personal before it can be social. Every prophet, every reformer, every revivalist had to meet God alone before he could help the multitudes. The great leaders who went on to turn thousands to Christ had to begin with God and their own soul. The plain Christian of today must experience personal revival before he can hope to bring renewed spiritual life to his church.

# What About
# Revival?—Part III

*Prayer Is Not Enough*

These words are addressed to those of God's children who have been pierced with the arrow of infinite desire, who yearn for God with a yearning that has overcome them, who long with a longing that has become pain.

"Blessed are those who hunger and thirst for righteousness,/ for they will be filled" (Matthew 5:6). Hunger is a pain. It is God's merciful provision, a divinely sent stimulus to propel us in the direction of food. If food-hunger is a pain, thirst, which is water-hunger, is a hundredfold worse, and the more critical the need becomes within the living organism the more acute the pain. It is nature's last drastic effort to rouse the imperiled life to seek to renew itself. A dead body feels no hunger and the dead soul knows not the pangs of holy desire. "If you want God," said the old saint, "you have already found Him." Our desire for fuller life is proof that some life must be there already. Our very dissatisfactions should encourage us, our yet unfulfilled aspirations should give us hope. "What I aspired to be, and was not, comforts me," wrote Browning with true spiritual insight. The dead heart cannot aspire.

In nature everything moves in the direction of its hungers. In the spiritual world it is not otherwise. We gravitate toward our inward longings, provided of course that those longings are strong enough to move us. Impotent dreaming will not do. The religious urge that is not followed by a corresponding act of the will in the direction of that urge is a waste of emotion. The awe-inspiring power of a discharge of lightning may dissipate itself in the atmosphere and accomplish nothing, while a flashlight battery may provide illumination for a miner hours on end. One is a dramatic display of immense power without direction and the other a quiet application of modest energy to an intelligent purpose.

It is my conviction that much, very much, prayer for and talk about revival these days is wasted energy. Ignoring the confusion of figures, I might say that it is hunger that appears to have no object; it is dreamy wishing that is too weak to produce moral action. It is fanaticism on a high level for, according to John Wesley, "a fanatic is one who seeks desired ends while ignoring the constituted means to reach those ends."

Granted that the man who seeks revival has stopped thinking in plurals and has narrowed his faith down to one single individual, himself, what then? How can he find that after which his soul is yearning? How can he cooperate with his hungers to the end that he may indeed be filled?

He must rid his mind of the false notion that prayer alone will bring the blessing. Normally all transactions between the soul and God are carried on by prayer. It is right and scriptural and according to the testimony of all the saints that any spiritual advance on any front, any deliverance, any purification, any enduement of power, comes by the prayer of faith. Our error is that we try to secure these benefits by prayer *alone*.

The correction of this error is extremely difficult for it entails more than a mere adjustment of our doctrinal beliefs; it strikes at the whole Adam-life and requires self-abnegation, humility and cross-carrying. In short it requires *obedience*. And that we will do anything to escape.

It is almost unbelievable how far we will go to avoid obeying God. We call Jesus "Lord" and beg Him to rejuvenate our souls, but we are careful to do not the things He says. When faced with a sin, a confession or a moral alteration in our life, we find it much easier to pray half a night than to obey God.

Intensity of prayer is no criterion of its effectiveness. A man may throw himself on his face and sob out his troubles to the Lord and yet have no intention to obey the commandments of Christ. Strong emotion and tears may be no more than the outcropping of a vexed spirit, evidence of stubborn resistance to God's known will. Jacob wrestled against the angel through one whole night. It was only after he had been defeated that he became the aggressor and refused to let go of God. Why did Jacob resist so long? Because he was ashamed to confess his name to the angel. When he finally broke down and admitted that he was the supplanter, the victory was won. He triumphed in defeat.

No matter what I write here, thousands of pastors will continue to call their people to prayer in the forlorn hope that God will finally relent and send revival if only His people wear themselves out in intercession. To such people God must indeed appear to be a hard taskmaster, for the years pass and the young get old and the aged die and still no help comes. The prayer meeting room becomes a wailing wall and the lights burn long, and still the rains tarry.

Has God forgotten to be gracious? Let any reader begin to obey and he will have the answer. "Whoever has my commands and obeys them, he is the one who loves me. He who loves me will be loved by my Father, and I too will love him and show myself to him" (John 14:21).

Isn't that what we want after all?

---

# What About
# Revival?—Part IV

*How to Have a Personal Revival*

I have previously shown that any Christian who desires to may at any time experience a radical spiritual renaissance, and this altogether independent of the attitude of his fellow Christians.

The important question now is, How? Well, here are some suggestions which anyone can follow and which, I am convinced, will result in a wonderfully improved Christian life.

1. Get thoroughly dissatisfied with yourself. Complacency is the deadly enemy of spiritual progress. The contented soul is the stagnant soul. When speaking of earthly goods Paul could say, "I have learned to be content"

(Philippians 4:11); but when referring to his spiritual life he testified, "I press on toward the goal" (3:14). "So stir up the gift of God that is in thee" (2 Timothy 1:6, KJV).

2. Set your face like a flint toward a sweeping transformation of your life. Timid experimenters are tagged for failure before they start. We must throw our whole soul into our desire for God. "The kingdom of heaven has been forcefully advancing, and forceful men lay hold of it" (Matthew 11:12).

3. Put yourself in the way of the blessing. It is a mistake to look for grace to visit us as a kind of benign magic, or to expect God's help to come as a windfall apart from conditions known and met. There are plainly marked paths which lead straight to the green pastures; let us walk in them. To desire revival, for instance, and at the same time to neglect prayer and devotion is to wish one way and walk another.

4. Do a thorough job of repenting. Do not hurry to get it over with. Hasty repentance means shallow spiritual experience and lack of certainty in the whole life. Let godly sorrow do her healing work. Until we allow the consciousness of sin to wound us, we will never develop a fear of evil. It is our wretched habit of tolerating sin that keeps us in our half-dead condition.

5. Make restitution whenever possible. If you owe a debt, pay it, or at least have a frank

understanding with your creditor about your intention to pay, so your honesty will be above question. If you have quarreled with anyone, go as far as you can in an effort to achieve reconciliation. As fully as possible make the crooked things straight.

6. Bring your life into accord with the Sermon on the Mount and such other New Testament Scriptures as are designed to instruct us in the way of righteousness. An honest man with an open Bible and a pad and pencil is sure to find out what is wrong with him very quickly. I recommend that the self-examination be made on our knees, rising to obey God's command-ments as they are revealed to us from the Word. There is nothing romantic or colorful about this plain, downright way of dealing with ourselves, but it gets the work done. Isaac's workmen did not look like heroic figures as they digged in the valley, but they got the wells open, and that was what they had set out to do.

7. Be serious-minded. You can well afford to see fewer comedy shows on TV. Unless you break away from the funny boys, every spiritual impression will continue to be lost to your heart, and that right in your own living room. The people of the world used to go to the movies to escape serious thinking about God and religion. You would not join them there, but you now enjoy spiritual communion with them in your own home. The devil's ideals, moral standards and mental attitudes

are being accepted by you without your knowing it. And you wonder why you can make no progress in your Christian life. Your interior climate is not favorable to the growth of spiritual graces. There must be a radical change in your habits or there will not be any permanent improvement in your interior life.

8. Deliberately narrow your interests. The jack-of-all-trades is the master of none. The Christian life requires that we be specialists. Too many projects use up time and energy without bringing us nearer to God.

If you will narrow your interests, God will enlarge your heart. "Jesus only" seems to the unconverted man to be the motto of death, but a great company of happy men and women can testify that it became to them a way into a world infinitely wider and richer than anything they had ever known before. Christ is the essence of all wisdom, beauty and virtue. To know Him in growing intimacy is to increase in appreciation of all things good and beautiful. The mansions of the heart will become larger when their doors are thrown open to Christ and closed against the world and sin. Try it.

9. Begin to witness. Find something to do for God and your fellow men. Refuse to rust out. Make yourself available to your pastor and do anything you are asked to do. Do not insist upon a place of leadership. Learn to obey. Take the low place until such time as God sees fit to

set you in a higher one. Back your new intentions with your money and your gifts, such as they are.

10.  Have faith in God. Begin to expect. Look up toward the throne where your Advocate sits at the right hand of God. All heaven is on your side. God will not disappoint you.

If you will follow these suggestions you will most surely experience revival in your own heart. And who can tell how far it may spread? God knows how desperately the church needs a spiritual resurrection. And it can only come through the revived individual.

# CHAPTER 6

# The Use and Abuse of Good Books— Part I

## *What Should a Book Do for Us?*

It is a doubtful compliment to a book to say that we found it so interesting that we "read it at one sitting." A book that can be so read is not likely to be the most helpful one.

The best book is the one that sets us off on a train of thought that carries us far away from and far beyond the book itself. Sometimes a single paragraph will accomplish this, or a single sentence; then we will be wise to close the book and let God and nature and our hearts be our teachers.

When the noted scholar Dr. Samuel Johnson

visited the king, the two sat for a while before the fire in silence. Then the king said, "I suppose, Dr. Johnson, that you read a great deal." "Yes, Sire," replied Johnson, "but I *think* a great deal more." One of the English poets—I believe it was Coleridge—boasted to a Quaker lady about his study habits. He began his studies the instant he got up in the morning: while he dressed he memorized poetry; he studied his Greek vocabulary while he shaved; and so to the end of the day. The lady was unimpressed. "Friend," she asked reproachfully, "when does thee think?"

Apart from technical information which, of course, must be received from others, a man can teach himself much more than he can learn from books. A good book should do no more than prime the pump. After that the water will flow up from within as long as we keep the handle working and long after the original cup of water has been forgotten.

All else being equal it is desirable that Christians, especially ministers of the gospel, should be widely read. It is a disagreeable experience to present oneself before a teacher for religious instruction and discover in less than three minutes that the said teacher should have changed places with his listeners and learned from them rather than they from him. If he is a humble man and sticks close to the small plot of ground with which he is familiar, he may, if he loves God and men, succeed in ministering to the spiritual needs of his flock. If, however, his ignorance is exceeded by his arrogance, then God help his hearers. If he boasts of his ignorance and scorns learning, show me the nearest exit! I can learn more from a child laughing on the lawn or a cloud passing overhead.

Another type of speaker that drives me out into the fresh air is the unco-learned who knows more than he can handle comfortably and has more big words than he knows what to say with. He looks at his hearers in a faraway detached manner and talks of matters remote from their interest and above their understanding. His vocabulary consists almost wholly of academic jargon. He is sure to try to establish a "frame of reference," and "think in terms of" while he exhorts his listeners (if they are still listening) to "live horizontally" instead of "vertically," or vice versa. The racy, colloquial language people understand is carefully avoided and an artificial argot that blocks communication studiously chosen. For the great majority of persons it amounts to hearing a sermon preached in Sanskrit. Learning that produces this effect must be classified as pseudo-learning and surely has nothing to recommend it.

The book that informs us without inspiring us may be indispensable to the scientist, the lawyer, the physician, but mere information is not enough for the minister. If knowledge about things constituted learning, the encyclopedia would be all the library one needed for a fruitful ministry. The successful Christian, however, must know God, himself and his fellow men. Such knowledge is not gained by assembling data but by sympathetic contact, by intuition, by meditation, by silence, by inspiration, by prayer and long communion. I therefore recommend reading, not for diversion, nor for information alone, but for communion with great minds. The book that leads the soul out into the sunlight, points upward and bows out is always the best book.

The man who can teach me to teach myself will help me more in the long run than the man who spoon-feeds me and makes me dependent upon him. The teacher's best service is to make himself unnecessary. The book that serves as a ramp from which my mind can take off is the best book for me. The book that follows me into the pulpit and intrudes itself into my sermon is my enemy and an enemy to my hearers. The book that frees me to think my own inspired thoughts is my friend.

# CHAPTER 7

# The Use and Abuse of Good Books— Part II

*Books Good and Bad*

D r. Samuel Johnson said that if a young man would acquire knowledge he should read five hours a day anything he felt inclined to read. This is not an exact quotation but is a fair summary of his words.

In its historic and literary context this might have been a wise bit of advice, but if by some flash of prophetic inspiration the great doctor could have foreseen the flood of printed matter that rolls from our modern presses each day, he would surely have qualified his famous dictum considerably.

"Read anything" becomes extremely harmful advice in 20th century America.

At a table where all the food is wholesome, "eat anything" may be safe counsel for the guests; but where some of the food is without nourishment and some is downright poisonous, it may be a counsel of death to those that follow it. And if we should exercise care in selecting matter to take into our stomachs, how much more important that we be most careful of the quality of matter we take into our minds. For it should always be remembered that a human soul may be destroyed through the mind as surely as a human body through the stomach.

I have never subscribed to the doctrine that we Christians should live in an intellectual vacuum, refusing to hear what the world has to say. A faith that must be "protected" is no faith at all. If I can retain my faith in Christ only by closing my mind against every criticism, I give proof positive that I am not well convinced of the soundness of my position. The soul that has had a saving encounter with God is sure beyond the possibility of a doubt. His happy testimony will be, "To the LORD I cry aloud,/ and he answers me from his holy hill./ I lie down and sleep;/ I wake again, because the LORD sustains me./ I will not fear the tens of thousands/ drawn up against me on every side" (Psalm 3:4–6). Such a man will not need to shield himself from the classics nor from comparative religions or philosophy or psychology or science. The Spirit bears witness to Christ deep within his consciousness. His heart knows, though his reason my not yet have caught up with his heart.

When a very young minister, I asked the famous holiness preacher, Joseph H. Smith, whether he would recommend that I read widely in the secular field. He replied, "Young man, a bee can find nectar in the weed as well as in the flower." I took his advice (or, to be frank, I sought confirmation of my own instincts rather than advice) and I am not sorry that I did.

John Wesley told the young ministers of the Wesleyan Societies to read or get out of the ministry, and he himself read science and history with a book propped against his saddle pommel as he rode from one engagement to another. Andy Dolbow, the American Indian preacher of considerable note, was a man of little education, but I once heard him exhort his hearers to improve their minds for the honor of God. "When you are chopping wood," he explained, "and you have a dull axe you must work all the harder to cut the log. A sharp axe makes easy work. So sharpen your axe all you can."

I hope my readers conclude right here that I have contradicted myself in the above paragraphs. It will indicate that they have been reading with their critical faculties awake. But actually there is no self-contradiction present. I have warned against harmful books and declare that there is no harm in reading in fields far removed from the standard evangelical meadows considered safe by the timid souls who think they must defend Christianity and protect the faithful from the effects of alien ideas. I'll explain.

By *harmful* books I do not mean those on a high intellectual level, such as the classics, poetry, history, political science and whatever falls within the category of the liberal arts. I mean cheap fiction (religious or secular), shallow religious chop suey such as is found in so many religious magazines, the world of religious trash designed to entertain the saints; I mean the self-glorifying religious adventure stories written by the brethren of the restless feet who refuse to take any responsibility or to stay in one place long enough to plant a single tree or lay a single foundation, but who always manage to spin an exciting yarn when they get back home. I mean the "digest" type of religious literature, precooked and predigested, to be ingested with a minimum of effort and in the shortest possible time. Such matter not only affords no nourishment for the soul, but its continuous use creates a parasitic mind in the reader, gives him a morbid appetite for wind and makes the reading of serious religious books not only distasteful but impossible.

I deliberately omit from my list of dangerous

books the vulgar and the unclean. I take it for granted that no Christian would stain his soul with such literary putrefaction. At least I am quite sure that no one who reads this page will need to be warned about such books.

---

# The Use and Abuse
# of Good Books—
# Part III

*Speed and Memorizing*

Abook is a reservoir in which the raw material of thought is stored; or, otherwise viewed, a channel through which ideas are piped from one mind to another. It is therefore not an end but a means only. In itself it is but a few ounces of paper and cloth and ink, the sum of which can be bought anywhere for a few cents.

It is necessary that we understand this, for some persons confuse the means with the end and by association come to attribute to a book powers almost magical. There are those who acquire books from a sort of compulsion, imagining that there is some kind of intellectual advantage in the mere fact of possession. Others seem to believe that they are the better for merely reading the book, as if its mysterious treasure passed into the mind as the eye travels over the page. I have seen men stroke and fondle a book with a kind of superstitious reverence as if they hoped that something wonderful would rub off on them by physical contact. The bibliophile who gloats over his volumes is no better off than the miser who, with drawn shades, counts his money over and over before returning it to its hiding place again. Books and money are alike in that they are useless when hoarded. Each has a purpose and is valuable only when allowed to fulfill that purpose.

The Greek moral philosopher, Epictetus, understood well the difference between means and end, and exhorted his listeners constantly to beware mistaking the one for the other. The wise old Stoic looked for results in the life and was not impressed by the number of books his students had read. "Show me then your progress in this point," he demanded. "As if I should say to a wrestler, 'Show me your muscle' and he should answer, 'See my dumbbells.' Your dumbbells are your own affair. I desire to see the *effect* of them."

That brings us naturally to inquire whether or not there is any advantage in the new stepped-up speed reading advocated so widely today and, conversely, whether there is any real disadvantage in slow reading habits.

The advocates of speed reading like to tell of such men as Theodore Roosevelt who, it is said, could sweep his eyes down a page and grasp what was written there at a glance and almost without effort. Such a man is too rare to set the pace for the rest of us. His kind occurs about as frequently as an albino crow and for all practical purposes may be passed over as having no meaning for the ordinary student. If our only desire were to pack information into our heads, then we might profit by the ability to race over the page. Since, however, we seek in books more than information, such ability is surely of questionable worth. If reading has for one of its most important benefits intellectual communion with superior souls, then rapid reading is a positive disadvantage. The slow, leisurely walk through the woods will teach us more than a sprint that makes observation impossible; and the quiet, deliberate perusal of a great book, with many stops and frequent retracings of our steps, will always be best. In that way we learn from the book and from ourselves at the same time. Briefly, no one should worry about his reading rate. Just find your natural easy pace and let who will race past you. Remember the hare and the tortoise.

Closely related to the idea of reading rate is that of the relative importance of memorizing—whether we should try to memorize, and if so, how much.

Certain cultures have stressed memorization to a point where education consists largely in learning by rote a few of the classics. This was true in ancient China, in India, and I believe is still true in some parts of the world, such as Arabia. Missionaries tell us of the remarkable ability to memorize possessed by some of the Orientals, an ability which they find they cannot possibly match.

About this two things may be said: One, that great skill in memorizing is found almost exclusively among peoples where books are scarce and where a certain limited few important classics are about all the reading matter required for an education as understood by those peoples. In the English-speaking world of today we have available not only everything that has ever been written in our mother tongue, but everything that has ever been written in any language, done for us in English translation. In the face of such a mountain of books, memorizing on any wide scale will be seen to be altogether impossible.

The second thing is that excessive memorization kills the impulse to think independent thoughts and makes us into tape recording machines full of other men's words but without a vital idea of our own. It is my considered opinion that a book that has fed a great thought into my mind and inspired me to explore new ideas on my own has done vastly more for me than the book I have memorized from cover to cover.

My own method is to confine my memorization to the Scriptures and the great hymns. I memorize passages of Scripture so I can use them in my sermons and meditate on them as I travel. And I like to store the great hymns in my mind to sing under my breath anywhere under any circumstances at any time. Further than that I do not give myself too much concern about memorizing.

---

# CHAPTER 9

# The Use and Abuse of Good Books— Part IV

## *Reading for Verbal Skill*

God has honored human speech by using it as a medium through which to express His message of salvation, first in the inspired Scriptures and afterwards in a thousand languages and dialects among the nations of mankind. Language is the mighty organ upon which may be played the joyous oratorio of redemption for the blessing of men and for the high honor of God.

Among the countless gifts of God, one of the most precious to us is our beautiful, expressive English tongue. That such a gift should be neglected by busy men and women in their wild race to make a living is at least understandable, if unfortunate; but that it should be neglected as well by the ministers of the sanctuary is not only impossible to understand but completely inexcusable.

For the very reason that God has committed His saving truth to the receptacle of human language, the man who preaches that truth should be more than ordinarily skillful in the use of language. It is necessary that every artist master his medium, every musician his instrument. For a man calling himself a concert pianist to appear before an audience with but a beginner's acquaintance with the keyboard would be no more absurd than for a minister of the gospel to appear before his congregation without a thorough knowledge of the language in which he expects to preach.

There have been extraordinary situations where God has blessed a halting and broken message to the edification of the hearers, but these must be recognized as instances of providential overrulings and not as the operation of the highest will of God. Under an abnormal set of circumstances God moved Balaam's ass to speak with enough eloquence to convict a renegade prophet and rate being quoted in the Bible. But surely no one would cite this as proof that religious teachers should not concern themselves about their skill in the use of language. Those holy men who spoke as they were moved by the Holy Spirit, and whose writings constitute the sacred Scriptures, were one and all master of their medium. Each one brought to the service of God a remarkable facility in the use of words. Some were writers of the first magnitude and deserve a place among the great literary figures of all time.

If such a high standard was required of those who recorded the Holy Scriptures, dare we who expound them bring to our task anything short of the best and most perfectly developed gifts possible? We may lack the artistry of a David or the eloquence of an Isaiah, but there is no reason why we cannot acquire a skill in the use of words that will enable us to say anything we want to say with clarity. It will take hard work and long application, but if we begrudge these, we should get out of the ministry. No true prophet has ever been afraid of hard work.

Children learn to speak by imitation. Whether they grow up to use poor or good English depends altogether upon the quality of English spoken by those around them. Adult students of the art of speech never advance far beyond the childhood technique of unconscious imitation. We tend to imitate the speech of those we associate with, and particularly those we admire. For this reason it is vitally important that we cultivate the fellowship of the masters of English.

Intimate association with a great literary fig-
ure within the covers of a book will do more to
teach us skill in the use of words than twenty
years' study of grammar could do. It is a
notorious fact that those who teach English in
our schools are frequently the worst possible
examples of their art. If you want heavy sled-
ding, read an essay written by a professor of
English. It is sure to be very correct and just as
sure to be very dry. Bone is jointed to bone
with anatomical precision, but there is no
breath nor hearing. The writer is grammar conscious and tone deaf. He is eager to have his
sentences parse correctly, but seems unable to
make them live.

Good speaking as well as good writing has its
pitch, its tempo, its balance and rhythm, its
tone and timbre. And these things cannot be
learned in the popular sense of the word; *they
can only be acquired by unconscious imitation*. If
we listen long and sympathetically to someone
who uses English with style and artistry, something of his art will seep through the pores of
our minds and improve our own style greatly.
And remember that reading is hearing with the
mind. We listen to a man when we read his
book with a congenial spirit.

Some of my younger readers may want to
know who the "masters" are to whom I have
referred, and what books I recommend to
develop verbal skill. Here are a few: John
Bunyan for simplicity; Joseph Addison for

clarity and elegance; John Milton for nobility and consistent elevation of thought; Dickens for sprightliness (start with the *Christmas Carol*); Bacon for conciseness and dignity.

In addition to these I would recommend Robert Louis Stevenson, John Ruskin, Thomas Carlyle, Nathaniel Hawthorne. Also the poetry of Wordsworth, Bryant, Blake, Keats and Shelley. Then to keep close to the modern mind, and for the sake of style only, we might read Pegler, "Red" Smith and Sidney Harris. *Time* magazine is slanted and somewhat on the frivolous side, but it is alive, and it will help us to avoid stodginess and literary cliches. For that reason I recommend it—in limited doses.

# chapter 10

# The Use and Abuse of Good Books— Part V

*If We Would Understand,
We Must BE and DO*

Through the foresight and zeal of certain publishers within the last few years many of the great religious classics of the past have been revived and made available to the Christian public in attractive editions. These have been mostly of two kinds, viz., the works of the Puritan divines and those of the mystic theologians and devotional writers from St. Augustine to John Woolman.

The great Puritan writers and those closely related to them in doctrine and spirit were the

spiritual forebears of our present day Fundamentalists, though candor requires that we
note that, for reasons that need not be
enumerated here, the noble fathers were not
able to beget sons equal to themselves.

The devotional works that have appeared
have been so varied as to make classification
difficult. Some of the great names are Meister
Eckhart, Bernard of Clairvaux, Jan van
Ruysbroeck, Michael Molinos, John of the
Cross, Thomas Traherne, Richard Rolle, William Law, Walter Hilton, Francis de Sales,
Jakob Boehme and Gerhart Tersteegen. To
those might be added the more familiar names
of Fenelon, Guyon and Thomas á Kempis.

To a large extent these were universal Christians who experienced the grace of God so
deeply and so broadly that they encompassed
the spiritual possibilities of all men and were
able to set forth their religious experiences in
language acceptable to Christians of various
ages and varying doctrinal viewpoints. Just as
a sincere hymn may strike a worshipful chord
common to all Christians, so these works of
devotion instantly commend themselves to
true seekers everywhere. There need only be
genuine faith in Christ, complete separation
from the world, an eager cleaving unto God
and a willingness to die to self and carry the
cross, and the Holy Spirit will introduce His
people to each other across the centuries and
teach them the meaning of spiritual unity and

the communion of saints.

What disturbs me is the sharp disparity between theory and fact in the reception given
these great spiritual classics by the rank and
file of evangelicals. Theoretically the people of
God should run to these books as a thirsting
stag runs to bury his muzzle in the cooling
stream; actually only a relatively few welcome
them. Most Christians find them dull, and even
though they may buy them, they seldom look
into them, and wonder how they got their
reputation as religious masterworks.

Why is this? Why do the majority of present
day Christians prefer shallow religious fiction?
Or uninspired Bible talks that never get beyond
the "first principles"? Or one-page daily devotions? Or watered-down Christian biography? I
think the reasons are two:

First, present day evangelical Christianity is
not producing saints. The whole concept of
religious experience has shifted from the
transcendental to the utilitarian. God is valued
as being useful and Christ appreciated because
of the predicaments He gets us out of. He can
deliver us from the consequences of our past,
relax our nerves, give us peace of mind and
make our business a success. The all-consum-
ing love that burns in the writings of an Augustine, a Bernard or a Rolle is foreign to the
modern religious spirit. Like understands like
and fails to comprehend what is unlike itself.
The tortoise finds the mockingbird dull. Esau

has no fellowship with Jacob. "The man without the Spirit does not accept the things that come from the Spirit of God, for they are foolishness to him, and he cannot understand them, because they are spiritually discerned" (1 Corinthians 2:14).

To come to our devotions straight from carnal or worldly interests is to make it impossible to relish the deep, sweet thoughts found in the great books we are discussing here. We must know their heart-language, must vibrate in harmony with them, must share their inward experiences or they will mean nothing to us. Because we are too often strangers to their spiritual mood, we are unable to profit by them and are forced to turn to one or another form of religious entertainment to make our Christianity palatable enough to endure.

Secondly, people are unable to appreciate the great spiritual classics because they are trying to understand them while having no intention to obey them. The Greek Church father, St. Gregory, said it better than I could, so we'll let him tell us: "He who seeks to understand commandments without fulfilling commandments, and to acquire such understanding through learning and reading, is like a man who takes shadows for truth. For the understanding of truth is given to those who have become participants in truth (who have tasted it through living). Those who are not participants in truth and are not initiated therein, when they seek this understanding, draw from it a distorted wisdom. Of such the apostle says, 'The natural man receiveth not the things of the Spirit,' even though they boast of their knowledge of truth."

In conclusion, we use books profitably when we see them as a means toward an end; we abase them when we think of them as ends in themselves. And for all books of every sort let us observe Bacon's famous rule: "Read not to contradict and confute, nor to believe and take for granted, nor to find talk and discourse, but to weigh and consider. Some books are to be tasted, others to be swallowed, and some few to be chewed and digested."

CHAPTER

11

---

# Who Does the Work
# of God?

In a close and final sense no one can do God's
work. Nor does He turn His work over to
others to do. He works *in* His people and
*through* them, but always it is *He* who works.

Jesus said, "My Father is always at his work
to this very day, and I, too, am working" (John
5:17); and Paul said, "It is God who works in
you to will and to act according to his good
purpose" (Philippians 2:13).

This is not to teach that men should not work.
One has but to run his eyes over the pages of
the Bible casually to become convinced that
God intends His people to work. He put the
man in the Garden of Eden "to work it and
take care of it" (Genesis 2:15). Our Lord was a
carpenter and He chose active men for His first
disciples. The book of Proverbs has some scath-

ing things to say about the sluggard who loafs away his days in careless indolence only to have poverty come upon him at last like an armed man (Proverbs 6:11).

Certain passages of Scripture, if carelessly read, might give the impression that God delegates some of His work to Christian leaders to do for Him as a manufacturer might sublet to others certain items in a contract; such, for instance, as First Corinthians 15:58, "Therefore, my dear brothers, stand firm. Let nothing move you. Always give yourselves fully to the work of the Lord, because you know that your labor in the Lord is not in vain." In First Corinthians 16:10 Paul says plainly that Timothy "is carrying on the work of the Lord, just as I am," but we must never understand from this that these men did a work of God apart. Rather they were the obedient instruments in whom and through whom God wrought His own work.

Any misunderstanding about this is cleared up by the explanation of Paul in Colossians 1:29, "To this end I labor, struggling with all his energy, which so powerfully works in me"; and First Corinthians 15:10, "I worked harder than all of them—yet not I, but the grace of God that was with me."

If this working, yet not working, doing God's work, yet not doing it, should seem to be confusing, remember there is a parallel for it in the well-known testimony of Paul in Galatians

2:20, "I have been crucified with Christ and I no longer live, but Christ lives in me." From all this I think we may draw the following conclusion: *We can no more do the work of God than we can live the life of God.* In the believing and surrendered soul, Christ lives His life again and continues to live it, and in the obedient, believing man, God will continue to work, reaching out and through the human instrument to accomplish His wonders among men.

It is critically important that we grasp this truth. Much religious work is being done these days that is not owned by our Lord and will not be accepted or rewarded in that great day. Superior human gifts are being mistaken for the gifts of the Holy Spirit, and neither they who exercise these gifts nor the Christian public before whom they are exercised are aware of the deception. Never has there been more activity in religious circles and, I confidently believe, never has there been so little of God and so much of the flesh. Such work is a snare because it keeps us busy and at the same time prevents us from discovering that it is our work and not God's.

"Nothing is wrought by creatures," said Meister Eckhart; "the Father works alone. The soul shall never stop until she works as well as God. Then she and the Father shall do His work together: she shall work as one with Him, wisely and lovingly. That we may be in unity with Him. God help us. Amen."

# chapter 12

# Not Too Many But the Wrong Kind

T he happiest man in the world," said a
well-known preacher some time ago, "is
the new convert before he has met too many
Bible teachers and seen too many church members."

Even after we have made what allowance we
must for the obvious irony in these words,
there still remains in them sufficient truth to
perturb the honest Christian soul more than a
little.

Surely one of the happiest persons in the
world should be the new convert. Has he not
found Him of whom Moses and all the
prophets did write? The spontaneous song that
bursts from his lips is likely to be:

Hallelujah! I have found Him

Whom my soul so long has craved.
Jesus satisfies my longings;
Through His blood I now am saved.

Old things pass away and all things become new. So brilliant is the contrast between the dark despair of but a few short hours ago and the new, bright world into which he has been thrust by the miracle of faith that every nerve and cell in his complex personality vibrates joyously. The testimony of many persons known for their poise and self-restraint has been that at the time of their first satisfying encounter with Christ the whole world took on a new luster. It is not unusual to hear people say that on the night of their conversion, the air smelled sweeter, the stars shone more brightly and all the common familiar objects of nature appeared to glow with a subdued light. And that these men and women were not the victims of a hallucination is proved triumphantly by the stability of their subsequent lives and the salty good sense manifest in all their religious attitudes.

The first half of our opening quotation, then, is so true as to need no verification. "The happiest man in the world is a new convert." But it is the last half that disturbs me. Why should a Bible teacher or a church member tend to destroy the joy of the new convert? Well, to be just to everyone I must assert positively that not all Bible teachers and church members would have such an adverse effect. I know Bible teachers who would delight in piling more fuel on the blazing altar of the young Christian's heart, and I know church members whose influence and example would be a source of great strength to his whole life. But I also know many of the other kind, the kind the young convert must actually climb over in his struggle to advance in the Christian life.

The way some Bible teachers injure the new convert is to take away his simplicity; and the way some church members do it is by disillusioning him—before he is ready for it.

The newborn Christian finds himself alive with a sweet, enjoyable kind of life that he accepts naively, almost unconsciously. To him everything is simple and immediate. He knows no intermediary. Christ is to him on an infinitely higher level what its mother is to a baby— warmth, nourishment, protection, rest and an object of satisfying affection.

Right here is where the wrong kind of Bible teacher can do his damage. The first thing he does is to destroy the new Christian's simplicity. He introduces something between the Christian and Christ. He makes him Biblo- centric instead of Christo-centric. (And there is a difference, let no one deceive you.) The Spirit- anointed Bible teacher will so teach the Word as to keep it transparent, so as to allow it to be what it always should be, a kind of burning bush which God indwells and out of which He shines in awesome splendor. The beholder sees the bush, it is true, but the object of his interest is the Presence, not the bush. The wrong kind of teacher gets so technical about the bush that the fire dims down and the light ceases to fall on the Christian's face.

That is what the gentle cynic meant when he said "before he has met too many Bible teachers."

As for "too many church members" spoiling the new Christian's happiness, it is the result of disillusionment pure and simple.

When we are first converted, especially if we come from a non-Christian background, we are likely to be almost too naive for our own good. The wondrous experience through which we have just passed, or perhaps I should say into which we have entered, has predisposed us to believe in everybody. Our trust in other Christians is likely to be boundless. That there could be hypocrites, double-minded professors, religious pretenders, carnal camp followers, never once enters our minds. The result is that our first encounter with a worldly church member comes as a frightful shock to our sensitive minds. Some never recover from this shattering of their confidence. They become religious cripples. Their growth is stunted and their usefulness destroyed, or at the least greatly hindered from that moment on.

That I speak truly here may be proved by everyday experience; but there is a more sure word of Scripture: "But if anyone causes one of these little ones who believe in me to sin [shall offend any one of these, KJV] it would be better for him to have a large millstone hung around his neck and to be drowned in the depths of the sea" (Matthew 18:6).

When we learn that the word *offend* actually means *cause to stumble* or *to sin*, we know how serious the whole thing is. Better to die than to imperil the faith of a weak disciple. Christ's words may mean more than that, but they can hardly mean less.

# CHAPTER 13

# Words without Meaning Are Idle Words

We Christians owe it to ourselves and to the human race to be above all persons, candid, downright and completely transparent. We must have no truck with fancy, but see to it that our religious talk hugs the facts as tightly as a glove and that our words always have some reality corresponding to them.

Over the years I have been disturbed more than a little by the vague unreality of much that I hear among religious people. This is not a charge of insincerity. I have no doubt of the sincerity of most religious persons. It is the lack of reality that disturbs me. Indeed the gravity of the situation is increased by the very earnestness with which many persons are occupied with unreality.

Religion stands at the top as being among all fields of human interest the one most addicted to words. Nowhere else are there so many words and so few deeds to support them. There is something about a religious gathering, and particularly about a church building, that produces in the worshiper a state of pleasant languor and suspends his critical faculties for the duration of the service. The average Christian goes to church expecting to hear certain words and phrases and the average preacher knows what they are. It does not matter too much in what order they occur, and if they should be spoken with a considerable degree of enthusiasm, so much the better; only let them be familiar and harmless. Nothing more is required or expected.

Religious people are psychologically conditioned to the trite phrase and the hackneyed expression. True, the stereotyped pattern varies slightly between different groups, but there would seem to be no reason why a clever speaker could not preach tonight to Calvinists, tomorrow to Arminians, the next day to Pentecostals, the next to Holiness people, and successively to Separatists and Adventists, and preach acceptably to each one by the simple expedient of finding out what they were conditioned to expect and giving it to them. A clever man could do this, I say, but an honest man would not. And the reason the clever man could do it is that the ability to create a specific pattern of words is all that is demanded of the speaker. That he may be talking about something he has never experienced to people who do not understand him seems not to occur to anyone. The reassuring drone of safe and familiar religious phrases is enough to give the listeners an enjoyable sense of well-being. The absence of reality is not even noticed.

A Christian is among other things a witness, and as such he speaks of those things which he has personally experienced. The Bible was, for the most part, written by men who saw and heard certain great realities and reported on them. "I saw" and "I heard" are familiar Old Testament expressions, and the New Testament literally pulsates with life and experience. John's vivid words are a sample:

> That which was from the beginning, which we have heard, which we have seen with our eyes, which we have looked at and our hands have touched—this we proclaim concerning the Word of life. The life appeared; we have seen it and testify to it, and we proclaim to you the eternal life, which was with the Father and has appeared to us. We proclaim to you what we have seen and heard. (1 John 1:1–3)

Now, while we cannot project ourselves backward through time and walk again in Galilee with Christ and His disciples, we can by faith actually experience "the substance of things hoped for"; we can have every sufficient "evidence of things not seen" (Hebrews 11:1, KJV); we can taste "the powers of the coming age" (6:5); we can "know" and "comprehend"; we can have the inner witness, the spiritual illumination that brings out the typography of the kingdom of God as clearly as any earthly landscape is revealed by the rising sun. Then every word will be like a sharp, clear shadow thrown by the objects on the terrain, not to stand in place of reality, but to outline it and set it in relief.

A word is valid only when it refers to some reality in the mind of the user. It must submit to definition as used by the speaker. Its dictionary meaning cannot save it from semantic fraud. It must have a real meaning in its limited context at a given time. By this test an alarmingly great amount of our religious talk is phonetic breath, no more.

At the risk of shocking some tender-minded persons, I venture to list here a few words and phrases that to millions of evangelical Christians have no longer an identifiable content and are used merely as religious sounds without any relation to reality. They *have* meaning, and they are good and sacred words, but *they have no meaning as used by the speaker and as heard by the listener in the average religious gathering.* Here they are: *victory, heart and life, all out for God, to the glory of God, receive a blessing, conviction, faith, revival, consecration, the fullness of God, by the grace of God, on fire for God, born again, filled with the Spirit, hallelujah, accept Christ, the will of God, joy and peace, following the Lord*—and there are scores of others.

We have reared a temple of religious words comfortably disassociated from reality. And we will soon stand before that just and gentle Monarch who told us that we should give an account of every idle word. God have mercy on us.

# CHAPTER 14

# A Needed
# Reformation

A great deal can be learned about people by observing whom and what they imitate. The weak, for instance, imitate the strong; never the reverse. The poor imitate the rich. The self-assured are imitated by the timid and uncertain, the genuine is imitated by the counterfeit, and people all tend to imitate what they admire.

By this definition power today lies with the world, not with the church, for it is the world that initiates and the church that imitates what she has initiated. By this definition the church admires the world. The church is uncertain and looks to the world for assurance. A weak church is aping a strong world to the amusement of intelligent sinners and to her own everlasting shame.

Should any reader be inclined to dispute these conclusions, I ask him to take a look around. Look into almost any evangelical publication, browse through our bookstores, attend our youth gatherings, drop in on one of our summer conferences or glance at the church page of any of our big city newspapers. The page that looks most like the theatrical page is the one devoted to the churches, usually appearing on Saturday. And the similarity is not accidental, but organic.

This servile imitation of the world is for the most part practiced by those churches that claim for themselves a superior degree of spirituality and boldly declare their adherence to the letter of the Word. In fact, neither the old-line ritualistic churches nor those that are openly modernistic have been as guilty of such flagrant world-worship as the gospel churches have.

The arguments brought forward in defense of this gross sellout are so thin as to need no refutation. They are but a lame effort to excuse a procedure that has been adopted from weakness and uncertainty, never from vision or spiritual enlightenment.

Once the prophet, the apostle, the reformer, saw a vision or heard a voice, or in later times had an encounter with God through the holy Scriptures and went out firm and sure to declare the Word of the Lord. Now we watch the world to get our next cue and when we have been tipped off as to what our latest "burden of the Word of the LORD" (Zechariah 12:1, KJV) shall be, we rush out and breathlessly declare the expected message as if we had been with Moses on Mount Sinai. It takes a war, an election, race tensions or an outbreak of juvenile crime to afford subject matter for our modern prophets. Not the Word of the Lord, but *Life* and *Time* and the roving radio commentator set the pace and determine our preachment. The world always moves first and the church comes meekly after, trying pitifully to look and sound like her model and at the same time maintain a weak religious testimony by inserting a dutiful commercial now and then to the effect that everybody ought to accept Jesus and be born again.

Secularized fundamentalism is a horrible thing, a very horrible thing, much worse in my opinion than honest modernism or outright atheism. It is all a kind of heart heterodoxy existing along with creedal orthodoxy. Its true master may be discovered by noting whom it admires and imitates. The test is, *Whom do these Christians want to be like? Who excites them and makes their eyes shine with pleasure? Whom go they forth to see? Whose techniques do they borrow?* Never the meek soul, never the godly saint, never the self-effacing, cross-carrying follower of Jesus. Always the big wheel, the celebrity, the star, the VIP—provided of course that these persons have given a "testimony" in favor of

Christ somewhere in the midst of the fleshly, vain world of artificial lights and synthetic sounds which they inhabit.

The sad thing about all this is its effect upon a new generation of Christians. Whole companies of young people are growing up who have known nothing else but the degenerate brand of Christianity now passing for the religion of Christ. They are the innocent victims of a condition which they did not help to create. Not they but a spiritually emasculated leadership must answer for their plight.

What is the remedy? It is simple. A radical return to New Testament Christianity both in message and in method. A bold repudiation of the world and a taking up of the cross. Such a return on any wide scale will mean a reformation of vast proportion. Some that are now high will be brought low and many of the humble will be exalted. It will mean a moral revolution. How many are willing to pay the price?

# CHAPTER 15

# Perpetual Sacrifice or Perpetual Efficacy?

In a friendly conversation with a Catholic priest I learned from the lips of this appointed spokesman of the Roman Church the philosophy of the Mass.

He started with the blood offering of Abel and traced the practice of propitiatory sacrifice down through the Scriptures to the cross. "There must always be a sacrifice," he said, "and in the Mass the sacrifice is repeated each time the bread and wine are consecrated on the altar. At each celebration of the Mass the sacrifice of Christ is repeated."

If the Mass rests upon the notion of the perpetual sacrifice then its foundation is only sand, for the New Testament is very clear that Christ's sacrifice is a once-for-all act and can never be repeated. Whatever tradition and dogma may say, thus saith the Lord.

> And by that will, we have been made holy through the sacrifice of the body of Jesus Christ once for all.
>
> Day after day every priest stands and performs his religious duties; again and again he offers the same sacrifices, which can never take away sins. But when this priest had offered for all time one sacrifice for sins, he sat down at the right hand of God. (Hebrews 10:10–12)

And if that is not plain enough the inspired writer further says, "Because by one sacrifice he has made perfect forever those who are being made holy" (verse 14); and, "where these have been forgiven, there is no longer any sacrifice for sin" (verse 18).

The teaching of the New Testament is not that there is a perpetual sacrifice, but that *there is one sacrifice of perpetual efficacy*. The thought that Christ's sacrifice needs to be repeated is obnoxious to the spirit of biblical theology and an affront to the tears and sweat and blood and death of the Lamb of God.

Obviously our Catholic friends are in serious error here, and the kind thing is not that we in the name of tolerance smile away their error, but that we point it out and try to correct it.

# chapter 16

# The Corrosive Effects of a Fretful Spirit

The Holy Spirit in Psalm 37:1 admonishes us to beware of irritation in our religious lives:

> Do not fret because of evil men
> or be envious of those who do wrong.

The word "fret" comes to us from the Anglo-Saxon, and carries with it such a variety of meanings as bring a rather pained smile to our faces. Notice how they expose us and locate us behind our disguises. The primary meaning of the word is *to eat*, and from there it has been extended with rare honesty to cover most of the manifestations of an irritable disposition. "To eat away; to gnaw; to chafe; to gall; to vex; to worry; to agitate; to wear away"; so says Webster, and all who have felt the exhausting, corrosive effects of fretfulness know how accurately the description fits the facts.

Now, the grace of God in the human heart works to calm the agitation that normally accompanies life in such a world as ours. The Holy Spirit acts as a lubricant to reduce the friction to a minimum and to stop the fretting and chafing in their grosser phases. But for most of us the problem is not as simple as that. Fretfulness may be trimmed down to the ground and its roots remain alive deep within the soul, there growing and extending themselves all unsuspected, sending up their old poisonous shoots under other names and other appearances.

It was not to the unregenerate that the words "Do not fret" were spoken, but to God-fearing persons capable of understanding spiritual things. We Christians need to watch and pray lest we fall into this temptation and spoil our Christian testimony by an irritable spirit under the stress and strain of life.

It requires great care and a true knowledge of ourselves to distinguish a spiritual burden from religious irritation. We cannot close our minds to everything that is happening around us. We dare not rest at ease in Zion when the church is so desperately in need of spiritually sensitive men and women who can see her faults and try to call her back to the path of righteousness. The prophets and apostles of

Bible times carried in their hearts such crushing burdens for God's wayward people that they could say, "My tears have been my food day and night" (Psalm 42:3), and "Oh that my head were a spring of water/ and my eyes a fountain of tears! I would weep day and night/ for the slain of my people" (Jeremiah 9:1). These men were heavy with a true burden. What they felt was not vexation but acute concern for the honor of God and the souls of men.

By nature some persons fret easily. They have difficulty separating their personal antipathies from the burden of the Spirit. When they are grieved they can hardly say whether it is a pure and charitable thing or merely irritation set up by other Christians having opinions different from their own.

Of one thing we may be sure; we can never escape the external stimuli that cause vexation. The world is full of them and though we were to retreat to a cave and live the remainder of our days alone, we still could not lose them. The rough floor of our cave would chafe us, the weather would irritate us and the very silence would cause us to fret.

Deliverance from a fretting spirit may be by blood and fire, by humility, self-abnegation and a patient carrying of the cross. There will always be "evildoers" and "workers of iniquity," and for the most part they will appear to succeed while the forces of righteousness will seem to fail. The wicked will always have the money and the talent and the publicity and the numbers, while the righteous will be few and poor and unknown. The prayerless Christian will surely misread the signs and fret against the circumstances. That is what the Spirit warns us against.

Let us look out calmly upon the world; or better yet, let us look down upon it from above where Christ is seated and we are seated in Him. Though the wicked spread himself like "a green tree in its native soil" (Psalm 37:35), it is only for a moment. Soon he passes away and is not. But "the salvation of the righteous comes from the LORD;/ he is their stronghold in time of trouble" (verse 39). This knowledge should cure the fretting spirit.

# No Sin Is Private

No sin is private. It may be secret but it is not private.

It is a great error to hold, as some do, that each man's conduct is his own business unless his acts infringe on the rights of others. "My liberty ends where yours begins" is true, but that is not all the truth. No one ever has the right to commit an evil act, no matter how secret. God wills that men should be free, but not that they be free to commit sin.

Sin is three-dimensional and has consequences in three directions: toward God, toward self and toward society. It alienates from God, degrades self and injures others. Adam's is the classic example of a secret sin that overflowed to the injury of all mankind. History provides examples of persons so placed that their sins had wide and injurious effect upon their generation. Such men were

Nero, Napoleon, Hitler and Stalin, to name but four. These men dramatized the destructive social results of personal sin; but every sin, every sinner injures the world and harms society, though the effects may be milder and less noticeable.

When Sigmund Freud's mother rubbed her sweaty hands together, her curious son noticed how little pellets of dirt rolled together and fell to the floor. This rather disgusting sight is said to have started the young Sigmund thinking in directions that finally led to his world-shaking theories that turned certain time-honored concepts of human life upside down. Someone with a bit of imagination has wondered where popular psychology would be today if Mrs. Freud had kept her hands clean!

Have you ever wondered what the world would be like today if Napoleon had become a Christian when he was in his teens? Or if Hitler had learned to control his temper? Or if Stalin had been tenderhearted? Or if Himmler had fainted at the sight of blood? Or if Goebles had become a missionary to Patagonia? Or if the 12 men in the Kremlin should get converted to Christianity? Or if all businessmen should suddenly turn honest? Or if every politician should stop lying?

Only God could reconstruct the world and allow for such reversals of fact; but anyone can tinker at it theoretically. Had Hitler, for instance, been a good and gentle man, six million

Jews now dead would be living (making allowance for a certain few who would have died in the course of nature); had Stalin been a Christian, several million Russian farmers would be alive who now molder in the earth. And consider the thousands of little children who died of starvation because one man had a revengeful spirit; think of the millions of displaced persons who wander over the earth even today unable to locate mother or father or wife or child because men with hate in their hearts managed to get into places of power; think of the young men of almost every nation, sick with yearning for home and loved ones, who guard the empty wastes and keep watch on frozen hills in the far corners of the earth, all because one ruler is greedy, another ambitious; because one statesman is cowardly and another jealous.

To come down from the bloody plains of world events and look nearer home, how many wives will sob themselves to sleep tonight because of their husband's savage temper; how many helpless, bewildered, heartbroken children will cower in their dark bedrooms, sick with shock and terror as their parents curse and shout at each other in the next room. Is their quarrel private? Is it their own business when they fight like animals in the security of their home? No, it is the business of the whole human race. Children to the third and fourth generation in many parts of the world will be

injured psychologically if not physically because a man and his wife sinned inside of four
walls. No sin can be private.

Coming still closer, we Christians should
know that our unchristian conduct cannot be
kept in our own back yard. The evil birds of sin
fly far and influence many to their everlasting
loss. The sin committed in the privacy of the
home will have its effect in the assembly of the
saints. The minister, the deacon, the teacher
who yields to temptation in secret becomes a
carrier of moral disease whether he knows it or
not. The church will be worse because one
member sins. The polluted stream flows out
and on, growing wider and darker as it affects
more and more persons day after day and year
after year.

But thanks be to God, there is a cure for the
plague. There is a balm in Gilead. "If we confess our sins, he is faithful and just and will for-
give us our sins and purify us from all
unrighteousness" (1 John 1:9).

# chapter 18

# Zeal: What Does It Prove?

I f we were to ask at random 100 religious persons to state what they considered to be the chief characteristics of a devout Christian, it is reasonably certain that about 90 percent of them would include zeal in the list. So high does that single quality rate among us as an external evidence of internal grace.

Now as I have pointed out before, when a notion gets too popular it is pretty certain to be questionable if not downright false. Ideas accepted uncritically are usually wrong in fact, or at least wrong as understood by the masses. Whatever can be passed lightheartedly from one person to another is either not true or, if true, it is truth out of focus. I believe our naive faith in the evidential value of zeal is entirely unfounded. It will not stand up under examination.

Zeal, according to Webster, means *ardor in the pursuit of anything; ardent and active interest; enthusiasm; fervor.* Surely this should describe a Christian, and the better the Christian the more accurately it should apply. The devout soul should and will be fervent. He will pursue the things of God actively and be enthusiastic in his cultivation of the spiritual life. In his attitude toward Christ he will manifest fervid love and burning devotion. So we would seem to go along with the majority who hold zeal to be a sure mark of godliness. But it is only seeming. We do not go along with them, and here are the reasons:

While the true Christian is zealous, it is altogether possible to be zealous and not be a Christian. Zeal proves only that the one who manifests it is healthy, energetic and actively interested in something. As far as my experience goes, the most zealous religionists of our day are the wrongly named Jehovah's Witnesses. If zeal indicates godliness, then these ardent devotees of error are saints of the first order, a notion that could hardly be entertained by anyone who knew them intimately. Next to them, in the degree of temperature they manage to generate over their religion, are the "Peace! It's wonderful" dupes of the little dark, lower-case god, Father Divine. They are ablaze with zeal, but they are nevertheless condemned on every page of the sacred Scriptures. Muslims pray oftener than the best Christians and are making converts to their faith in some parts of the world much faster than the followers of Jesus Christ. And who gave the world its most convincing demonstration of zeal in the last quarter century? Without doubt the Fascists, the Nazis and the Communists!

There are a certain number of persons that cannot rest until they are making a great noise and stirring up a world of dust. Their temperament demands that they be always burnt up about something. Their type of mind forbids that they let their friends and neighbors alone until they have come over on their side and gotten behind some sure-fire movement to save the world. They are perpetually dashing from door to door collecting signatures demanding the abolishment of this or the establishment of that. One such dear, tender-hearted little lady, deeply in love with the birds, appeared for years every time our state legislators met in Springfield and fervently pressed for a bill to muzzle all cats in the state! So zealous was she that the weary lawmakers finally surrendered to her pressure and passed the bill. (It was later vetoed by the then governor, Adlai Stevenson.)

The truth is that though all godly persons are zealous, not all zealous people are godly. The zeal that accompanies sanctity is rarely boisterous and noisy. So great was the zeal of our Lord that it was said to have eaten Him up, yet Isaiah said of Him: "He will not shout or cry out,/ or raise his voice in the streets./ A

bruised reed he will not break,/ and a smolder-
ing wick he will not snuff out." And it was He
who excoriated the zealots who compassed sea
and land to find one convert, only to make him
more evil than he was before.

Not the quantity of zeal matters to God, but
the quality. The significant question is not how
zealous is the Christian but why is he zealous
and to what does his zeal lead? To the church
at Laodicea our Lord said, "Be zealous, therefore, and repent" (Revelation 3:19, KJV). The
zeal that leads to penitence, restitution and
amendment of life is surely dear to God. The
ardor that drives a man to his knees in intercession for others was found in men like Moses,
Daniel and Ezra; but there is a kind of zeal that
gives to the world such misshapen religious examples as Joseph Smith and Mary Baker Eddy.

That many Christians in our day are
lukewarm and somnolent will not be denied by
anyone with an anointed eye, but the cure is
not to stir them up to a frenzy of activity. That
would be but to take them out of one error and
into another. What we need is a zealous hunger
for God, an avid thirst after righteousness, a
pain-filled longing to be Christlike and holy.
We need a zeal that is loving, self-effacing and
lowly. No other kind will do.

That pure love for God and men which ex-
presses itself in a burning desire to advance
God's glory and leads to poured-out devotion
to the temporal and eternal welfare of our fel-

low men is certainly approved of God; but the
nervous, squirrel-cage activity of self-centered
and ambitious religious leaders is just as certainly offensive to Him and will prove at last to
have been injurious to the souls of countless
millions of human beings.

# chapter 19

# Religion:
# No Substitute
# for Action

The supreme purpose of the Christian religion is to make men like God in order that they may act like God. In Christ the verbs *to be* and *to do* follow each other in that order.

True religion leads to moral action. The only true Christian is the practicing Christian. Such a one is in very reality an incarnation of Christ as Christ is the incarnation of God; not in the same degree and fullness of perfection, for there is nothing in the moral universe equal to that awful mystery of godliness which joined God and man in eternal union in the person of the man Christ Jesus; but as the fullness of the Godhead was and is in Christ, so Christ is in the nature of the one who believes in Him in the manner prescribed in the Scriptures.

God always acts like Himself wherever He may be and whatever He may be doing. When God became flesh and dwelt among us, He did not cease to act as He had been acting from eternity. "He veiled His deity but He did not void it." The ancient flame dimmed down to spare the helpless eyes of mortal men, but as much as was seen was true fire. Christ restrained His powers but He did not violate His holiness. In whatsoever He did He was holy, harmless, separate from sinners and higher than the highest heaven.

Just as in eternity God acted like Himself and when incarnated in human flesh still continued to be true to His holiness in all His conduct, so does He when He enters the nature of a believing man. This is the method by which He makes the redeemed man holy. He enters a human nature at regeneration as He once entered human nature at the incarnation and acts as becomes God, using that nature as a medium of expression for His moral perfections.

Cicero, the Roman orator, once warned his hearers that they were in danger of making philosophy a substitute for action instead of allowing it to produce action. What is true of philosophy is true also of religion. The faith of Christ was never intended to be an end in itself nor to serve instead of something else. In the minds of some teachers faith stands in lieu of moral conduct and every inquirer after God must take his choice between the two. We are presented with the well-known either/or: either we have faith or we have works, and faith saves while works damn us. Hence the tremendous emphasis on faith and the apologetic, mincing approach to the doctrine of personal holiness in modern evangelism. This error has lowered the moral standards of the church and helped to lead us into the wilderness where we currently find ourselves.

Rightly understood, faith is not a substitute for moral conduct but a means toward it. The tree does not serve in lieu of fruit but as an agent by which fruit is secured. Fruit, not trees, is the end God has in mind in yonder orchard; so Christlike conduct is the end of Christian faith. To oppose faith to works is to make the fruit the enemy to the tree; yet that is exactly what we have managed to do. And the consequences have been disastrous.

A miscalculation in laying the foundation of a building will throw the whole superstructure out of plumb, and the error that gave us faith as a substitute for action instead of faith in action has raised up in our day unsymmetrical and ugly temples of which we may well be ashamed, and for which we shall surely give a strict account in the day when Christ judges the secrets of our hearts.

In practice we may detect the subtle (and often unconscious) substitution when we hear a Christian assure someone that he will "pray over" his problem, knowing full well that he intends to use prayer as a substitute for service. It is much easier to pray that a poor friend's needs may be supplied than to supply them. James' words burn with irony:

> Suppose a brother or sister is without clothes and daily food. If one of you says to him, "Go, I wish you well; keep warm and well fed," but does nothing about his physical needs, what good is it? (2:15–16)

And the mystical John sees also the incongruity involved in substituting religion for action:

> If anyone has material possessions and sees his brother in need but has no pity on him, how can the love of God be in him? Dear children, let us not love with words or tongue but with actions and in truth. This then is how we know that we belong to the truth, and how we set our hearts at rest in his presence. (1 John 3:17–19)

A proper understanding of this whole thing will destroy the false and artificial either/or. Then we will have not less faith but more godly works; not less praying but more serving; not fewer words but more holy deeds; not weaker profession but more courageous possession; not religion as a substitute for action but religion in faith-filled action.

And what is that but to say that we will have come again to the teaching of the New Testament?

# chapter 20

# Hope: The Universal Treasure—Part I

## *The Preciousness of Hope*

Among those treasures with which we are all endowed by nature, hope stands by itself as being at once the most precious and the most treacherous.

Just because hope is so common we accept it as a matter of course, without realizing how precious it is. Without it life in a fallen world would be unbearable; without it the zest for living would disappear almost at once; without it one hour of adversity would break our spirits and drive millions to suicide. It is not too much to say that if all hope were destroyed within the human breast, the race of mankind would die out altogether in a very few years. Even the procreative drive and the instinct for self-preservation would hardly be strong enough to save from extinction a race from which all hope had fled.

Hope is a nurse and comforter and enables us to go on after every reason for going on has disappeared. Hope has sustained the spirit of a shipwrecked sailor and given him strength to stay alive through the long days that seemed years till help and rescue came; hope has steeled the patriot to fight on and win at last against overwhelming odds; hope has saved from insanity or suicide the prisoner in his lonely cell as he checked off the years and months and days on his homemade calendar; hope has enabled the sick or injured man to wait out the pain and the nausea till health returned and the suffering ended; hope has made light the feet of the traveler hurrying home in near exhaustion to the bedside of someone he loved.

In the dealings of God with men, hope has held a noble place. The expectation that Messiah would come cheered Israel in her years of victory and kept her from despairing in her periods of captivity and dispersal. Those who feared the Lord have often had rough going.

> They were stoned; they were sawed in two; they were put to death by the sword: They went about in sheepskins and goatskins, destitute, persecuted and

> mistreated—the world was not worthy of them. They wandered in deserts and mountains, and in caves and holes in the ground. (Hebrews 11:37–38)

That is a New Testament tribute to Old Testament saints; but the record of Christian times is fully as grim and sometimes worse. Only the strength of a great expectation enabled the suffering saints to hold out to the end. The cheerful hope of better days allowed them not only to endure the pain but to sing and rejoice in the midst of it.

So strong, so beautiful is hope that it is scarcely possible to overpraise it. It is the divine alchemy that transmutes the base metal of adversity into gold. In the midst of death Paul could be bold and buoyant because he had firm confidence in the final outcome. "For we who are alive are always being given over to death for Jesus' sake," he said, but his heart remained cheerful knowing that "our light and momentary troubles are achieving for us an eternal glory that far outweighs them all" (2 Corinthians 4:11, 17). His lovely little benediction pronounced over the Roman Christians shows how faith and peace and joy live with hope like four fair sisters dwelling in the same cottage: "May the God of hope fill you with all joy and peace as you trust in him, so that you may overflow with hope by the power of the Holy Spirit" (Romans 15:13).

Faith is confidence in the character of God, and hope is the sweet anticipation of desirable things promised but not yet realized. Hope is an electronic beam on which the Christian flies through wind and storm straight to his desired haven. To the child of God, hope is a gift from the heavenly Father "who loved us and by his grace gave us eternal encouragement and good hope" (2 Thessalonians 2:16).

The Christian's hope is sound because it is founded upon the character of God and the redeeming work of His Son Jesus Christ. For this reason Peter could call it "a living hope" (1 Peter 1:3). It is living because it rests on reality and not on fancy. It is not wishful dreaming but vital expectation with the whole might of the Most High behind it.

# CHAPTER 21

# Hope: The Universal Treasure—Part II

## *The Treachery of Hope*

In a previous piece I said that hope is unique in being at once the most precious and the most treacherous of all our treasures. I have shown that, as Goldsmith says,

> Hope, like the gleaming taper's light,
> Adorns and cheers our way.

But we do not listen long to the voice of the keen and experienced teachers of the race until we detect a note of bitterness when they speak of hope. Dryden says bluntly,

> When I consider life, 'tis all a cheat.

Yet fooled with hope, men favour
the deceit.

And the cynical La Rochefoucauld writes:
"Hope, deceitful as it is, serves at least to lead
us to the end of life along an agreeable road."

Why this contradiction? Why is hope thought
to be both good and bad, both cheerful and
deceitful? A little observation will show us why.

Hope has sustained the spirit of many a
shipwrecked sailor by painting for him a
tender picture of rescue and reunion with
loved ones, only to leave him at last to die of
thirst and exposure on the vast bosom of the
sea. Hope has kept many a prisoner believing
he could not hang, that a pardon would surely
come, and then stood calmly by and watched
him die at the end of a rope. Hope has cheered
a thousand victims of cancer and tuberculosis
with whispered promises of returning health
who were never again to know one single day
of health till they died. Hope has told the
mother that her son missing in action was surely alive, and kept her watching till the end of
her days for the letter that never came and that
never could come because the boy that might
have written it had long been sleeping in an
unmarked grave on a foreign shore.

Surely for the fallen sons of men, the Hindu
proverb is true: "There is no disease like hope."
Hope that has no guarantee of fulfillment is a
false friend that comforts us a while with flat-

tery and leaves us to our enemies. Expectation of a bright tomorrow when no such tomorrow can be ours will be bitterness compounded by despair in the day of the great reckoning.

Only a Christian has a right to hope, for only he has the power of God to give substance to his hope. The man who hopes in Christ is as safe as the rainbow-circled throne where sits the God who cannot lie. Such a man has a moral right to look upward and quietly wait for the fulfillment of every promise. Let him but see to it that his anticipations conform to the revealed Word of God and he has nothing to doubt or fear in life or in death. His loftiest flights of fancy cannot outsoar the promises of God to those that love Him and that hope in His mercy.

> Because God wanted to make the unchanging nature of his purpose very clear to the heirs of what was promised, he confirmed it with an oath. God did this so that, by two unchangeable things in which it is impossible for God to lie, we who have fled to take hold of the hope offered to us may be greatly encouraged. We have this hope as an anchor for the soul, firm and secure. It enters the inner sanctuary behind the curtain, where Jesus, who went before us, has entered on our behalf. He has become a high priest forever, in the order of Melchizedek. (Hebrews 6:17–20)

Hope without the great High Priest is a false hope. How dare they look forward with cheerful expectation of blessedness to come who are not protected by the oath nor held steadfast by the anchor? What is certain about human hopes? Yet millions go on assuming that all is well with their souls when they have never known the forgiving love of God nor felt the kiss of His approval. They nourish the flimsy hope that they are not so bad after all and that "God's a good fellow and 'twill all be well." The worldly minded hope that they are children of God. The impenitent and unrenewed dream of the reward of the righteous and those whose nature fits them for hell pensively hope that they will enter heaven at last.

Earth is bearable because there is hope. Hell is unendurable because all hope has fled. Heaven is eternal beatitude because hope is there in radiant fulfillment.

"For you have been my hope,/ O Sovereign LORD,/ . . ./ I will always have hope;/ I will praise you more and more" (Psalm 71:5, 14).

# CHAPTER 22

# The Church Wins a Pyrrhic Victory

About 300 B.C. a Greek king named Pyrrhus fought a battle with the Romans at
Heraclea. Pyrrhus won the battle but in doing
so he suffered such appalling losses as to more
than offset his gains.

Thus a victory that costs too much is often
called a Pyrrhic victory.

A news item from the Associated Press a
short time ago brought to mind King Pyrrhus
and his too-expensive military triumph. The
item had to do with the American Association
for the Advancement of Atheism which, with
its sister organizations, the Freethinkers of
America and the National Liberty League, rode
high and mighty in the 1920s and '30s.
Together they had scores of branches or chapters in the United States. Militant atheists and

agnostics lectured each week to hundreds of persons who paid to get in. Smith and his atheists were headline news. Clubs known as "Damned Souls" were not uncommon on the various college campuses throughout the country. God, the Church and the Bible were under constant attack by the all-conquering army of the godless. That was, say, 25 years ago.

Well, it seems that an AP religious writer the other day got to wondering what had happened to all the anti-God shouting and arm swinging of yesterday and set out to investigate. He hunted up the aging Charles Smith (now 79) and asked him how come? Where was everybody? And what had happened to the triumphant army of atheism? His answers are significant.

First, the anti-religion organizations have shrunk away to a shadow. No one will pay any more to hear an atheist talk and only a ragged handful will come to hear him, free for nothing. The oldest and most famous of the anti-God magazines is down to a mere 2,000 circulation. The tumult and the shouting have died and the few professional atheists and agnostics yet remaining cannot work up enough mad to attack anybody even if they could find anyone to attack. Christianity has won! The church has scored a victory over those "blatant infidels" against whom I used to hear the preachers declaim a few years ago.

Maybe so. But let's not declare a holiday just yet to celebrate our triumph. It could be a Pyrrhic victory.

Mr. Smith believes that true intellectual atheism is stronger than ever and he explains his apparent defeat in a way that should make every serious Christian squirm. Even granting that Smith is on the defensive and his explanation may need a bit of discounting, there is truth enough in his words to drive us to our knees in penitence and shame.

The reason organized atheism has petered out in recent years, says President Smith, is that there is no longer any sharp battle line drawn between the doctrines of atheism and those of the church. The preaching that once angered the atheists and brought them charging out against God and the Bible has pretty much disappeared. Hell fire, miracles, the necessity that men please Almighty God, are no longer a serious part of current Christian teaching. Christianity has been watered down until it is little more than "cheer 'em up stuff," as Smith calls it. Instead of trying to please God, Christians now try to please their fellow men. The kind of Christianity that is being propagated now is not radical enough to rouse an atheist to want to "free" people from it. This new sort of religion, says the old atheist, is "not so bad." Religion is now taking a more rational position and is less offensive to atheists, and the churches are little more than social centers.

So says the old AAAA president, and if that doesn't hurt enough he adds these terrible, stinging words: "Some of them," he says, referring to Christians, "are nearly as good as atheists."

For years I have watched misled Christians in their unholy effort to make friends with the enemy and to render the cross socially acceptable. A few prophets have written and preached against this outrageous sellout, but their words have gone unheeded. The leadership of the popular Christian movements has been and still is in the hands of persons who are blind to the meaning of the cross. That darkness and light cannot mingle never so much as occurs to them. They are busily engaged copying the world and trying to be like it as far as they dare. To be a Christian one need only "accept" Christ. That brings "peace of mind" and assurance of heaven. After that the cross has no meaning and Christ no authority. Compromise and collaboration are now the distinguishing marks of religion. To be relaxed and well adjusted to society is more important that to keep the commandments of Christ. The fawning, ingratiating spirit is the modern badge of saintliness. Between the world and the Christian there is no longer any great difference. And that not by accident. They planned it that way.

Yes, we have won a victory over the atheists. They no longer cause us any trouble. But subsequent developments will show that our triumph has cost us too much. It is a Pyrrhic victory.

# Let No One Rob You of Your Christian Confidence

One thing taught throughout the Bible, and particularly in the New Testament, is that the Christian life is a progression, a journey of the redeemed soul toward God.

Another is that Satan stands to resist every step and to hinder the journey in every way possible. To advance against his shrewd and powerful opposition requires faith and steadfast courage. The epistles call it "confidence."

In his Philippian epistle Paul declares his own determination to advance against all obstacles. He says in effect that while he is not yet perfect and has not yet attained unto the goal set before him, he is putting the past behind him psychologically as well as chronologically that he may go on to find in

Christ his all in all. "I press on toward the goal," he says, "to win the prize for which God has called me heavenward in Christ Jesus" (Philippians 3:14). Then with a fine disregard for apparent self-contradictions he urges, "All of us who are mature should take such a view of things" (3:15).

In the Hebrew epistle a great deal is said about the need for persistence in the Christian life. The converts were losing heart and the man of God sought to encourage them to "hold firmly till the end the confidence we had at first" (3:14). "So do not throw away your confidence," he exhorts them, "it will be richly rewarded" (10:35).

This concept of the Christian life as a journey to be taken, a growth to be attained, is being lost to us through two widely separated modern errors.

The first is that of the liberal, who cheerfully advises the unrenewed sinner to continue in the Christian life, overlooking the important fact that he has no life in which to continue. Where there has been no impartation of life to the soul of the man, growth and development are impossible. To assume that a saving act of God has been done in a man's heart when in reality no such act has been done is to set the soul of the man in mortal jeopardy and all but guarantee his final ruin.

The second error is found among us evangelicals. This error is the exact opposite of the liberal's, which assumes spiritual life to be present when it is not; this one assumes that life is not there when it is. Unless every Christian virtue is in the soul, it flatly denies that any virtue is there at all. It requires all babies to be born full grown, and all pilgrims to reach their destination the same moment they set out on their journey. Those who hold this error seem possessed by a desperate hope that if they can shatter all faith and shake every Christian loose from his confidence they can bring about a revival. As they see it, no one is where he should be and will never arrive there until he admits that he has been deceived about himself up to now and has only just this minute seen the true light.

Once while listening to a man reproach, disparage and scold an assembly of Christians with whom he was only slightly acquainted and whose personal lives he had no way of appraising, I asked myself some questions, the answers to which up to this point I have not received. Since they bear directly on the matter here being discussed I want to list them. Perhaps some reader can answer them for me. Here they are:

Why do some preachers—

1. To take us on in the Christian life, begin by trying to prove that we have not started yet?

2. To emphasize a truth, assume or assert that everyone but them is ignorant of it?

3. To stir us to more praying, assume that we

never pray at all?

4. To make us feel penitent, imply that we had a fierce family quarrel just before we left for church?

5. To bring conviction of sin on an audience, act wise and mysterious and subtly suggest that there is deep and grave hidden evil present somewhere?

6. Create invidious comparisons, as for example: "You can preach about the deeper life all you will; I believe in foreign missions"; or "You may run to and fro over the earth engaged in foreign missions; I believe in love as the only way to please God." This is dishonest and confusing, but it does disturb the tenderhearted saints and bring them to the altar. I wonder if that is not the real purpose of it after all.

There comes a time when the true believer must take his stand on the oath and covenant of God and refuse to be shaken. He must lift high his happy affirmation, not in arrogance, but in faith and in deep humility. Perhaps his declaration of independence will go something like this:

I am not yet perfect, but I thank God and my Lord Jesus Christ that I am done with the past and I do now trust in my Savior for full deliverance from all my sins. I cannot pray like Daniel, but I shall never cease to praise God that He inclines His ear to me. I am not as wise as Solomon, but I glory in this, that "I know whom I have believed, and am convinced that he is able to guard what I have entrusted to him for that day" (2 Timothy 1:12). I have not the gifts of Moses or Isaiah or John, but I'll be everlastingly grateful that I have been given the moral perception to understand and appreciate such men as these. I am not what I want to be, but thanks be to God that I do want to be better than I am; and I am sure that "He who began a good work in [me] will carry it on to completion until the day of Christ Jesus" (Philippians 1:6).

Here I stand. I can do nothing else, so help me God.

# CHAPTER 24

# The Causes
# of Religious
# Confusion—Part I

## *Those Confused Intellectuals*

W e human beings can get confused so
easily that it might almost be said that
we brought into the world with us an inborn
ability to get mixed up.

It is a bit disconcerting to note that religion as
it is understood and practiced generally among
allegedly civilized men, instead of clearing up
our heads and putting things back in focus, appears actually to add to the number of things to
get confused about.

Now I well know that "religion that God our
Father accepts as pure and faultless" (James

1:27) is a clarifying and sobering agent. Christ reduced all commandments to one—that is, the love of God and man. He was Himself the simplest and most unified Man that ever lived, and always He saw things steadily and saw them whole. Except for that one awful moment in the garden when He prayed in an agony of bloody sweat, He evinced no trace of perplexity throughout His entire life. His heart was aglow with a love so warm that it drove out fear from the hearts of his hearers and drew to Him the weak, the timid and the self-condemned; yet, for all the hot fire in His heart, His mind was completely cool. Under every stress and pressure He was poised, calm and self-assured. He contributed nothing to the world's confusion, but He has done much to dispel it.

Having as the High Priest of our profession the incarnation of all divine wisdom and having as our source book of religious knowledge the holy Scriptures, the soundest and saltiest work ever written, why do we tend so easily to become confused about things spiritual? I believe the causes are four, and I propose to state them in this and the next chapters.

The first cause of religious confusion is our failure to understand that the truth as it is in Christ Jesus is a moral and spiritual thing and not something intellectual merely. Let a man approach the burning bush of divine truth with the desire to grasp it in his hand and the intensity of the fire will blind his eyes and cauterize his hands and face to the point of insensibility. Before the awesome vision of revealed truth, the human intellect should kneel and hide its face in trembling adoration. Because Moses was afraid to look upon God, the Lord could speak to him face to face as a man speaks to his friend; but God hides His face from the man who does not instinctively hide his own.

Intellectual pride, then, with its corollary, irreverence, is one cause of religious confusion. Satan's original doctrine, "You will be like God, knowing . . ." (Genesis 3:5) has been accepted by millions of religious persons through the centuries and commands a big following today even among professedly orthodox Christians. In spite of all Christ said while among men and all His inspired apostles wrote after His ascension, we seem never to learn that the inner essence of truth cannot be apprehended by the mental faculties. We still come at the awesome supernatural reality headfirst.

There has emerged lately in American Christianity a school of religious thought conceived in intellectual pride and dedicated to the proposition that everything of value in the Christian faith can be reduced to philosophical terms and understood by the human mind. The notion seems to be that anything God can utter we can comprehend, allowing possibly for the need of a little divine aid with the heavier stuff.

The brethren who are promoting this movement seem to feel that the trouble with evangelicalism is that it is not scholarly enough, that it cannot state itself in scientific terms. They appear to be chagrined by the chuckles of the learned liberals at the allegedly ignorant fundamentalists and have been needled into an attempt to prove that we evangelicals are not so dumb after all. They hope to make their point by equating Christian theology with Greek philosophy and the findings of modern science, and demonstrating that if the truth were known the Christian revelation is just good clean reason, nothing more. I pass over the pretty obvious fact that there is in all this more than a trace of the taint of mind-worship. And am I just seeing things or do I detect a deep and painful inferiority complex on the part of these apostles of evangelical-rationalism? But I won't call attention to it. I know how they feel.

Well, I believe these brethren are wrong. I believe they are as badly mixed up and confused as the peddlers of old wives' tales in Paul's day or the snake handlers of our own Ozark Mountains—only, of course, in a different and more respectable way. If they succeed in reducing Christianity to a philosophical proposition, they will do more damage to the true faith of Christ than liberalism, Catholicism and Communism combined.

But there is some hope. Invariably the newly learned, like the newly rich, overdo everything, and that is just what the evangelical-rationalists are doing. They forget that Moses, David, our blessed Lord Himself, John, Luther, Wesley, Bunyan, Schopenhauer, William James (to bring together a few very different but very effective teachers), could state their doctrines in language as simple as childhood talk and as clear as distilled water. These modern teachers aren't so easy to comprehend. They write in an academic jargon that only another of them can understand. At the rate they are going it will take at least one generation for their teaching to filter down to the man on the street and the worshiper in the pew. And maybe that is good after all.

# CHAPTER 25

# The Causes of Religious Confusion—Part II

*Lack of Love, Unbelief and Nonobedience*

I said that the causes of religious confusion were four, and I named misunderstanding of the nature of truth as one of them.

The others are lack of love, unbelief and non-obedience.

"Wisdom is a loving spirit," says the *Wisdom of Solomon*. "He guides the humble in what is right/ and teaches them his way" (Psalm 25:9), says David, the father of Solomon, and these set forth a truth which the whole Bible joins to celebrate; namely, that love and wisdom are forever joined and that soundness of moral judgment is for the meek alone. The humble, loving heart intuits truth as the Scriptures reveal it and the Holy Spirit illuminates it. The Spirit will not enlighten an unloving mind; and without His enlightenment the mysteries of Christian truth must forever remain a stranger to us.

To the loving mind God gives the power of immediate apprehension, and to none other. The theologian who is only a theologian must work out the teachings of the Scriptures as a child works out a jigsaw puzzle, fitting piece to piece with painstaking labor till at last he has a body of doctrine bearing some resemblance to the Biblical revelation. The difficulty (and the source of confusion) is that certain pieces will fit anywhere and others nowhere, so they may be forced into place or tossed back in the box at the whim of the student. But where love and illumination are, the picture always comes out right. *The Spirit says one thing to all loving hearts.*

Now lest I be misunderstood and so succeed only in confusing things still further, let me assure my readers that I am and have always been a staunch advocate of theology, and regularly teach doctrine systematically in pursuance of my pastoral calling. I joyfully recognize that there is an outline of divine truth fitted to the human mind and intended by its Author to be received by it. I think no one can become a strong Christian who is not a theologian of some sort, but it is altogether possible to be a theologian and not be a Christian at all. Bible doctrine without love is but a shadow of truth; doctrine held in love is very truth indeed, and we dare not allow ourselves to be satisfied with anything less.

Another source of religious confusion is unbelief. The writer to the Hebrews attributed Israel's failure to benefit by the truth to a breakdown in their faith. "But the message they heard was of no value to them, because those who heard did not combine it with faith" (Hebrews 4:2). The thought of holding holy truth in unbelief is a frightening thing. For the unbelieving mind to tinker with the truth of God is as terrible as was the unauthorized act of Saul when in fear and unbelief he offered a burnt offering at Gilgal. "I thought, 'Now the Philistines will come down against me at Gilgal, and I have not sought the LORD's favor.' So I felt compelled to offer the burnt offering" (1 Samuel 13:12). So the king explained his act, but there is something spine-chilling about it all. An unholy man tried to do a holy act and tragedy followed. From that hour Saul's life degenerated till at last, deserted and terrified, he died by his own hand.

The last cause I shall name is nonobedience. Truth is given to be believed and obeyed. Certain truths can only be believed, the reason being that they are revelations of fact and contain no command or instruction to be carried out. Other truths must be obeyed or for the hearer they have no meaning.

"I will come back" (John 14:3) is a statement of fact which cannot in the nature of it be obeyed; there is nothing in it to obey; it can only be believed. "Go and make disciples of all nations" (Matthew 28:19) is a command which can only be obeyed. It is addressed to the will, and the only proper response is obedience. We cannot possibly discharge our obligation to such a passage by trying in some dubious manner to "believe" it, though I am sure many try to do just that. Is it any wonder that confusion arises?

We will go far to simplify our religious concepts and unify our lives if we remember these four points: First, truth is a spiritual entity and can be grasped in its inner essence only as the Spirit of truth enlightens our hearts and teaches us in the deep, mysterious recesses of our souls. Secondly, since God is love we must surrender ourselves to love or we can never know the truth of God in its higher meaning. Thirdly, we must come to the Word with the simple faith of a child, ready to believe it whether we can understand it or not. And lastly, we must obey the truth as we see it, trusting God with the consequences.

# chapter 26

# The Problem of Numbers

The question of numbers and their relation to success or failure in the work of the Lord is one that disturbs most Christians more than a little.

On the question there are two opposing schools of thought. There are Christians, for instance, who dismiss the whole matter as being beneath them. These correspond to the lovers of high-brow music who firmly refuse to admit that there is anything of any real value other than that composed by Bach, Beethoven and Brahms. They know they are in the minority and glory in the fact, for in their opinion it is a very, very superior minority and they look down their noses at all who enjoy anything less complicated than a symphony.

Of course this is cultural snobbery and tells

us a lot more about such persons than they would care to have us know. They remind one of the unco-learned of whom Colton wrote,

> So much they scorn the crowd that
>     if the throng
> By chance go right, they purposely
>     go wrong.

Now among religious persons I have met a few who are guilty of a kind of spiritual snobbery of which they are doubtless wholly unaware. These have recoiled so violently from popular, cheap-Jack Christianity that they simply have no longer any sympathy with crowds. They prefer to sit around the Lord's Table in a select and tight little circle, admiring the deep things of God and, I very much fear, admiring themselves a wee bit also. This is a kind of Protestant monasticism without the cowl and the beads, for it seeks to preserve the faith of Christ from pollution by isolating it from the vulgar masses. Its motives may be commendable, but its methods are altogether unscriptural and its spirit completely out of mood with that of our Lord.

The other and opposite school is the most vocal and has by far the largest following in gospel circles today. Its philosophy, if it can be called a philosophy, is that "we must get the message out" regardless of how we go about it. The devotees of this doctrine appear to be more concerned with quantity than with quality. They seem burned up with desire to "bring the people in" even if they have not much to offer them after they are in. They take inexcusable liberties both with message and with method. The Scriptures are *used* rather than expounded and the Lordship of Christ almost completely ignored. Pressure is exerted to persuade the people (who, by the way, come to the meetings with something else in mind altogether) to accept Christ, with the understanding that they shall then have peace of mind and financial prosperity, not to mention high grades in school and a low score on the golf course.

The crowds-at-any-price mania has taken a firm grip on American Christianity and is the motivating power back of a shockingly high percentage of all religious activity. Men and churches compete for the attention of the paying multitudes who are brought in by means of any currently popular gadget or gimmick ostensibly to have their souls saved, but, if the truth were told, often for reasons not so praiseworthy as this.

Now the serious Christian wants to escape both extremes. Yet he is much concerned about the whole matter of numbers and is eager to find the will of God for his life and ministry. Should he go out for larger crowds or accept smaller ones as the will of God for him? Does success in the Lord's work depend upon numbers? Is it possible to make up in quantity what is lacking in quality and so accomplish the same result?

Perhaps an illustration or two might help. If our country should be visited by a famine and you were put in charge of feeding the starving in your section of the city, would numbers matter? Most surely they would. Would it not be better to feed five hungry children than two? Would you not feel obligated to feed hundreds rather than tens, thousands rather than hundreds? Certainly you would. Or if a ship sank and your church were given a rescue boat, would numbers mean anything? Again the answer is yes. Would it not be better to save 10 than two, 100 than 50?

So with the work of God. It is better to win many than few. Each lost one brought home increases the joy among the angels and adds another voice to the choir that shall sing the praises of the Lamb. Plainly Christ when He was on earth was concerned about the multitudes. And so should His followers be. A church that takes no interest in evangelism or missions is sub-normal in every way and desperately in need of revival.

Our constant effort should be to reach as many persons as possible with the Christian message, and for that reason numbers are critically important. But our first responsibility is not to make converts but to uphold the honor of God in a world given over to the glory of fallen man. No matter how many persons we touch with the gospel we have failed unless, along with the message of invitation, we have boldly declared the exceeding sinfulness of man and the transcendent holiness of the Most High God. They who degrade or compromise the truth in order to reach larger numbers, dishonor God and deeply injure the souls of men.

The temptation to modify the teachings of Christ with the hope that larger numbers may "accept" Him is cruelly strong in this day of speed, size, noise and crowds. But if we know what is good for us, we'll resist it with every power at our command. To yield can only result in a weak and ineffective Christianity in this generation, and death and desolation in the next.

# CHAPTER
## 27

---

# Not Papal
# Infallibility, But
# the Witness

In a recent letter a man from Jamestown, NY, quoted a statement from an editorial, "Three Degrees of Religious Knowledge," which appeared in these columns July 25, and asked for clarification.

The quotation was taken from that part of the editorial dealing with the third degree of knowledge: ". . . it is knowledge by direct spiritual experience . . . Since it was not acquired by reason operating on intellectual data, the possibility of error is eliminated."

The letter comments on this as follows: "This statement seems to me to parallel the Roman Catholic doctrine of papal infallibility. I was always taught that the holy Scriptures are the only rule of faith and life. My observation has

been that most of the false cults base their so-
called doctrines and revelations on personal
spiritual experience. I would appreciate your
further clarification on this editorial statement
. . . defining the boundaries with which 'direct
spiritual experience' can be depended upon
without danger of departure from the revealed
Word of God as contained in the holy Scriptures and as projected in the earthly life of
Christ."

This matter deserves further explanation and
I'll be glad to make it.

In my editorial I said that there are three
degrees of knowledge open to Christians. The
first is the common knowledge shared with all
normal persons, namely, the data furnished by
the senses and by reason operating upon such
data. This embraces all knowledge of natural
things from the first scrap of knowledge enjoyed by an hour-old baby to the highest
reaches of scientific information acquired by
the pooled efforts of the race.

The second is the knowledge received by
faith. It consists of data given by divine revelation and received by the believing mind
without proof. It is taken on trust and cannot in
the very nature of it be demonstrated as being
true. Were proof possible then it would belong
in the first category and faith would be unnecessary.

The third kind of knowledge is that given by
direct spiritual experience. This differs radically

from both of the others. It has nothing to do with the senses and so is not physical or natural data. It has nothing to do with ethics or doctrine and so is not moral or theological knowledge. I do not believe that God teaches doctrine by direct unmediated experience. The exact opposite is true. The Scriptures are the source of all rational knowledge about moral and religious things, except those things that are revealed by nature as mentioned in Psalm 19:1–4 and Romans 1:19–20, and they are few and inadequate.

Knowledge by spiritual experience is not mental, it is intuitive. It is consciousness, it is acquaintance with something or someone by direct awareness. It might help the reader to understand what we mean by such words as "awareness" and "consciousness" if he were to ask himself how he knows he exists, how he knows he is himself and not someone else, how he knows he is alive and not dead. The answer is simply that he "knows" these things by conscious awareness of which reason is no part. Let him attempt to prove to himself that he exists, for instance, and he will find that the "he" who is doing the demonstrating must first be *aware* that he exists before he can begin to prove that he does.

When the French philosopher, Descartes, sought to get to the root of all knowledge he thought away all accepted facts, went back till he found the one irreducible element of knowledge that could not be challenged and came up with his celebrated *Cogito, ergo sum,* "I think, therefore I am." But let no one imagine for a moment that with his little syllogism Descartes went all the way back. He did nothing of the kind. The truth is that he was by intuition aware of his existence before he ever began to notice that he was thinking. His self-knowledge antedated thought and all he did was to prove to reason that he existed by proof that it could understand: "I think, therefore I am."

This illustrates but does not explain what we mean by religious knowledge by direct spiritual experience. Stated in other language this means simply that there is at the root of true religion an inward *witness,* an *awareness* of God and Christ at the farthest-in core of the renewed Christian's spirit given to him by the Spirit of God. This experience results from faith in and obedience to the Scriptures. It is the end result of Bible doctrine but it is not that doctrine. It is a consciousness of God and spiritual things too deep and wonderful to utter or even think.

If this sounds too extreme or mystical let me remind my readers that it was once an accepted and expected phenomenon in most Protestant churches. In happier and holier times conversion was held to be (among other blessed things) an immediate acquaintance with God in living, spiritual experience. This came about as the result of the Word preached in the power of the Spirit.

And let's remember one thing more. Even today there are those who can testify that they too know what I am talking about here. We do not need to appeal to the dead past for support of our teaching. God still has His thousands who know what the inner witness is.

# CHAPTER 28

# The Gift of Prophetic Insight Imperative Today— Part I

A prophet is one who knows his times and what God is trying to say to the people of his times.

What God says to His Church at any given period depends altogether upon her moral and spiritual condition and upon the spiritual need of the hour. Religious leaders who continue mechanically to expound the Scriptures without regard to the current religious situation are no better than the scribes and lawyers of Jesus' day who faithfully parroted the Law without the remotest notion of what was going on around them spiritually. They fed the same diet to all and seemed wholly unaware that there was such a thing as meat in due season. The prophets never made that mistake nor wasted their efforts in that manner. They invariably spoke to the condition of the people of their times.

Today we need prophetic preachers; not preachers of prophecy merely, but preachers with a gift of prophecy. The word of wisdom is missing. We need the gift of discernment again in our pulpits. It is not ability to predict that we need, but the anointed eye, the power of spiritual penetration and interpretation, the ability to appraise the religious scene *as viewed from God's position*, and to tell us what is actually going on.

There has probably never been another time in the history of the world when so many people knew so much about religious happenings as they do today. The newspapers are eager to print religious news; the secular news magazines devote several pages of each issue to the doings of the church and the synagogue; a number of press associations gather church news and make it available to the religious journals at a small cost. Even the hiring of professional publicity men to plug one or another preacher or religious movement is no longer uncommon; the mail is stuffed with circulars and "releases," while radio and television join to tell the listening public what religious people are doing throughout the world.

Greater publicity for religion may be well and I have no fault to find with it. Surely religion should be the most newsworthy thing on earth, and there may be some small encouragement in the thought that vast numbers of persons want to read about it. What disturbs me is that, amidst all the religious hubbub, hardly a voice is raised to tell us what God thinks about the whole thing.

Where is the man who can see through the ticker tape and confetti to discover which way the parade is headed, why it started in the first place and, particularly, who is riding up front in the seat of honor?

Not the fact that the churches are unusually active these days, not what religious people are doing, should engage our attention, but *why* these things are so. The big question is: Why? And no one seems to have an answer for it. Not only is there no answer, but scarcely is there anyone to ask the question. It just never occurs to us that such a question remains to be asked. Christian people continue to gossip religious shoptalk with scarcely as much as a puzzled look. The soundness of current Christianity is assumed by the religious masses as was the soundness of Judaism when Christ appeared. People know they are seeing certain activity, but just what it means they do not know, nor have they the faintest idea of where God is or what relation He has toward the whole thing.

What is needed desperately today is prophetic

insight. Scholars can interpret the past; it takes prophets to interpret the present. Learning will enable a man to pass judgment on our yesterdays, but it requires a gift of clear seeing to pass sentence on our own day. One hundred years from now historians will know what was taking place religiously in this year of our Lord 1956; but that will be too late for us. We should know right now.

If Christianity is to receive a rejuvenation, it must be by other means than any now being used. If the Church in the second half of this century is to recover from the injuries she suffered in the first half, there must appear a new type of preacher. The proper, ruler-of-the-synagogue type will never do. Neither will the priestly type of man who carries out his duties, takes his pay and asks no questions, nor the smooth-talking pastoral type who knows how to make the Christian religion acceptable to everyone. All these have been tried and found wanting.

Another kind of religious leader must arise among us. He must be of the old prophet type, a man who has seen visions of God and has heard a voice from the Throne. When he comes (and I pray God there will be not one but many), he will stand in flat contradiction to everything our smirking, smooth civilization holds dear. He will contradict, denounce and protest in the name of God and will earn the hatred and opposition of a large segment of

Christendom. Such a man is likely to be lean, rugged, blunt-spoken and a little bit angry with the world. He will love Christ and the souls of men to the point of willingness to die for the glory of the One and the salvation of the other. But he will fear nothing that breathes with mortal breath.

This is only to say that we need to have the gifts of the Spirit restored again to the Church. And it is my belief that the one gift we need most now is the gift of prophecy.

# CHAPTER 29

# The Gift of Prophetic Insight Imperative Today— Part II

In the previous chapter I said that truth should not be passed out indiscriminately, but suited to the circumstances and needs of the hearers.

From the prophets we learn this and from the apostles, as well as from our Lord Himself. These were never bound by a mechanical religious "curriculum" which dictated unintelligently that certain doctrines were to be taught at certain times regardless of conditions. They prescribed truth as a divine medicine to be proclaimed with emphasis when the needs of the people called for it. They preached hope when the morale of the nation was low, obedience when the people grew careless, purity when their morals began to sag, humility when they became proud and repentance when they fell into sin. All was in accord with the total body of revealed truth, but the moral skill of these men of God enabled them to fit the message to conditions. Otherwise a vast amount of truth could have been wasted and a world of prayer and hard labor rendered ineffective.

Today the religious situation cries out for the skilled moral physician who can diagnose our ills and prescribe wisely for our cure. It is not enough simply to repeat correct doctrinal cliches. It is imperative right now that we have the benefit of the piercing discernment of the Spirit. We must not only know what God has said; *we must hear what God is now saying.*

No matter how sincere they may be, ministers without discernment are sure to err. Their conclusions are inevitably false because their reasoning is mechanical and without inspiration. I hear their error in our pulpits and read it in our religious periodicals; and it all sounds alike: revived churches engage in foreign missions; hence let us plunge into missionary activity and spiritual refreshing is sure to follow. The healthy church wins souls; let us begin to win souls and we will surely be revived. The early Church enjoyed miracles, so let's begin to expect mighty signs and wonders and we will soon be like the early Church. We have neglected the "social implications" of the gospel; let us engage in political activities and charitable endeavors and all will be well again.

Miserable counselors these, and physicians of no value. Their advice is not only poor; it is spiritually damaging.

What doctor in his right mind would tell a patient dying of tuberculosis, "Healthy men play football; go out and play ball and you will regain your health"? Such advice given under such circumstances would reveal only that effect was being mistaken for cause; and that is exactly what is happening these days in religious circles. *The effects of revival are being mistaken for the causes of revival.* And this to the confusion of everyone concerned and to the effective blocking of the spiritual refreshing for which so many are praying.

The critical need in this hour of the church's history is not what it is so often said to be: soul-winning, foreign missions, miracles. These are effects, not causes. The most pressing need just now is that we who call ourselves Christians should frankly acknowledge to each other and to God that we are astray; that we should confess that we are worldly, that our moral standards are low and we are spiritually cold. We need to cease our multitude of unscriptural activities, stop running when and where we have not been sent, and cease trying to sanctify carnal projects by professing that we are promoting them "in the name of the Lord" and "for the glory of God." We need to return to the *message, methods* and *objectives* of the New Testament. We need boldly and indignantly to cleanse the temple of all that sell cattle in the holy place, and overthrow the tables of the money-changers. *And this must be done in our own lives first and then in the churches of which we are a part.*

Christ told His disciples to tarry in Jerusalem until they had been endued with power from on high. This can only mean that He will not entrust His work to the unready and the unqualified. It is infinitely more important that we should be prepared for service than that we should win someone else to our subnormal spiritual condition. Soul-winning by persons who have not met the test of obedience to the Word of Christ must inevitably produce other professing Christians of the same spiritual stripe. Missions carried on by persons not spiritually endued can but transplant an effete Christianity on a foreign shore, for be sure that no church founded in a heathen land will be any better than the spiritual lives of those who founded it.

Real repentance will result in purified hearts and sanctified lives. A hard and determined return to the pattern shown us in the mount will bring the smile of God upon our efforts. Then we shall experience not less soul-winning, but more. Then we shall have not fewer missionary activities, but more. Then whatever we do shall prosper (Psalm 1:3), and God shall be glorified in everything at home and abroad.

# CHAPTER 30

# Optimist or
# Pessimist?

Immediately following the first World War, a wave of pessimism swept over the literate world.

What the cause was I shall not go into here but, whatever it was, the intellectual mood of the '20s and '30s was thoroughly despondent. Materialism, pessimism, cynicism and skepticism were the four horsemen of those gloomy decades and they rode forth conquering and to conquer.

The scientists were materialistic, the philosophers skeptical, the novelists and biographers cynical and almost everyone pessimistic. Even the interpreters of prophecy were apprehensive, for they saw in the capture of Jerusalem by the British and the rise of the Roman Empire under Mussolini evidence of the nearness of the tribulation days, the coming of Antichrist and the collapse of civilization. About the only religionists on the Protestant side who managed to retain a little optimism were the liberals ("modernists" they were called in those days), and they were cheerful for a wrong reason. Out of the poetic passages of a Bible, in which they no longer believed, they wove delicate daisy chains, which have long since withered, and crocheted pretty religious doilies of which they are not now exactly proud and which they would willingly forget but cannot because their handiwork is still to be found among us—on the 17 cent bargain table of the second-hand bookstores.

The close of World War II saw a radical change in the religious mood, especially on the part of the masses. It was a complete reversal. Religion came into its own. Faith became once more intellectually respectable and people stopped being ashamed to admit that they believed in God. Evangelicalism and the world wept briefly on each other's shoulders, kissed, shook hands and became friends. The church discovered that she could use a good many of the world's ideas and the world found that religion was a useful technique for achieving desired ends. The ox and the ass, as well as the lion and the lamb, romped together as they had not done since Luther nailed his theses on the door of the church at Wittenberg and launched the Reformation.

Over the last few years the world has gone on to woo the Church (about like water woos a duck!) and has won her heart and hand in what seems to be a case of true love. The honeymoon is still on and the church is now the pampered bride of the world. And what a dowry she has brought to her sensuous and drooling lover! An impenitent and unregenerate populace buys religious books by the millions, to the delight of the profit-hungry publishers. Movie stars now write our hymns; the holy name of Christ sounds out from the gaudy jukebox at the corner pool hall, and in all-night stomp sessions hysterical young people rock and roll to the glory of the Lord.

Today dark-browed Pessimism has gone out of vogue and her happy and responsible sister Optimism has come in to take her place. Christianity is now conceived as fun and the only cross is the one on which Jesus died several hundred years ago. Christ's yoke is not only easy, it is downright thrilling. His burden is not only light, it is jaunty. The church goes along with everything and stands against nothing—until she is convinced that it is the safe and popular thing to do; then she passes her courageous resolutions and issues her world-shaking manifestoes—all in accord with the world's newest social venture, whatever it may be.

The notion that Christians should always be optimistic and congenial is heresy pure and simple. An ill-founded optimism may, under certain conditions, be extremely harmful. A Christian is not obliged to be either pessimistic or optimistic or glad or sad or positive or negative after a preconceived rule of philosophy. He should (and will if he is Spirit-taught) reflect the will of God in any given situation. His one concern is with God's will. His one question in any set of circumstances is "What does God think of this?" To him nothing else matters. What the current popular attitude may be is of no importance to him. He will approve or disapprove altogether as the written Word and the indwelling Spirit indicate. Religious vogues, passing moods or popular notions will affect him not at all. His heart is fixed, trusting in the Lord.

This rather rigid attitude will, in a world like ours, quite naturally work against the one who holds it and earn him a reputation as a pessimist. People like the man who agrees with them, even if a day later they change their minds and require him to change his, too. This inconsistency they laugh off as an amiable weakness, and why be so pious about it anyway?

Well, the sons and daughters of eternity care very little about this maypole dance of popular favor. Like the water bird on the shore of the lake at the approach of winter, they feel within them a strong instinct to migrate. They expect before long to take off on a journey and they're not coming back soon. So whether they leave behind them a reputation for pessimism or optimism is of little consequence to them. They are, however, eager to be remembered as children of God and followers of the Lamb. That's all that matters to them.

# We Are All Heretics
by Nature

We are all heretics by nature and take to
error as instinctively as ducks take to
water.

This does not mean that natural theology is
wholly false, for the heavens declare the glory
of God and the visible universe shows His eternal power and Godhead. Add to these the
presence in the human heart of that light that
lights every man that comes into the world,
and you have the source of a certain body of
truth known more or less clearly by the whole
human race.

The knowledge thus received, however, is inadequate; it forms little more than a frame for
the total picture. The details are all unknown
and undiscoverable, so that we must depend
upon divine revelation as given in the holy

Scriptures to fill in the particulars and render the picture intelligible. The brush of the Holy Spirit labors to complete the work and to show every hill and rock and tree and blade of grass, each in its proper relation to everything else.

Until the full light of God's inspired Word floods down upon the religious landscape, almost everything is obscure and indistinct. The finest minds see things that are not there and fail to see the things that are. This inability to make out the details is a frustrating thing to persons of a strong religious bent and results in a lot of guessing and theological improvising. Such persons demand to know, and though they neglect or reject the holy Scriptures they *will* know, regardless, in some manner satisfying to themselves.

Bible lovers have been blamed for being excessively dogmatic and it may be that they sometimes are. I do not wish to justify a spirit of cocksureness wherever it may be found, but the certainty of the believer may be understood when it is remembered that it springs from his faith in the Scriptures as the full and true revelation of the mind of God to men. His dogmatism has back of it the strong "thus saith the Lord" of prophet and apostle. My own experience has taught me, however, that the most stubborn dogmatism is found not among those who quote the Bible to support their convictions, but among those who quote no one and claim for their spiritual authority nothing higher than their own opinions.

It is more than a little strange that persons who modestly decline to risk an opinion on matters that do not touch them at all closely, such as philosophy or science for instance, are often ready and eager to pronounce with finality on religion which above all else is vital to their welfare for this world and that which is to come. This follows the popular notion that everyone is capable of discovering for himself the true way to heaven and that one man's belief is as good as another's in any kind of weather. A second tenet in this creed is that no one has the right to question the belief of anyone else or to try to influence him in any way in religious matters. This leads naturally to the third tenet which is that we should practice complete tolerance toward every expression of religious belief, however base or ill-founded it may be, and accept it as someone's way of worshiping God even if it isn't ours.

All this has about it a certain savor of charity and slips well off the lips of politicians, who are forced to try to please everyone, and liberal ministers who find it profitable to do so. But the man who has knelt before the burning bush or heard the sound of thunder on the mount can never bring himself to sell out his soul in that manner. The man who has walked beside the sea and has heard the voice of Jesus saying "No one comes to the Father except through me" (John 14:6), can ever get the consent of his heart thus to trifle with religion. He has been smitten with the love of God and the wonder of the cross and he can never again be tolerant in things that touch his soul and the souls of his fellow men. He will live beside, be patient with, minister to, pray for and love any religionist of whatever color or creed from a cardinal to a medicine man from the long grass, but never will he compromise the truth to stay on good terms with anyone. He may die for men, but he will never trifle with them.

However unpopular we may become as a result, we must cling to the knowledge that all men are heretics by nature and can never know redeeming truth till they are enlightened from above by and through the inspired revelation we call the Scriptures. We are never kind to our neighbor when for the sake of sweet charity we smile away his perilous error and let him go unrebuked and uncorrected. The sons of light have an overwhelming obligation to the children of darkness. The lighthouse keeper dare not compromise with the storm; neither dare the light become friendly with the darkness.

The temptation to create our own creed and settle religious questions out of our own heads is as great in the pastor's study as in the corner tavern. No man knows enough to be sure he is right about divine things until he has submitted his ideas to the test of the Scriptures. Intelligence is not enough, nor experience nor brilliance. The Word of God is the final court of appeal. "I gain understanding from your precepts;/ therefore I hate every wrong path" (Psalm 119:104).

# CHAPTER
## 32

# The Shadow of
# Consequences

There is a close cause-and-effect relationship between deeds and consequences. No right-thinking person would try to deny this.

The whole scheme of rewards and punishment is a solid and substantial part of the belief of both Jews and Christians, as well as of many moral philosophers and of religions other than the Judeo-Christian. The human race at first was put on probation with the words, "but you must not eat from the tree of the knowledge of good and evil, for when you eat of it you will surely die" (Genesis 2:17). This is truth so generally accepted by Christians everywhere as to call for no further comment here.

To live our lives reverently in the fear of God and in view of eternal consequences is right and good, *but to live our moral lives in fear of tem-*

*poral consequences is an evil, a great and injurious evil for which not one shred of justification can be found.* Yet the shadow of the fear of consequences lies dark across the church today and its blight is seen almost everywhere.

Moral decisions should be made in view of moral consequences, never in fear of the effect such decisions may have upon our economic or social future. The wisest of the Greeks said, "A man who is good for anything ought not to calculate the chance of living or dying; he ought only to consider whether in doing anything he is doing right or wrong." It is more than a little embarrassing that an uninspired Stoic should see what so few of us Christians, with all our claims to superior religious experience, seem unable to understand.

It is doubtful whether we can be Christian in anything unless we are Christian in everything. To obey Christ in one or two or ten instances and then in fear of consequences to back away and refuse to obey in another is to cloud our life with the suspicion that we are only fair-weather followers and not true believers at all. To obey when it costs us nothing and refuse when the results are costly is to convict ourselves of moral trifling and gross insincerity.

The temptation to gear our lives to social consequences is frightfully strong in a world like ours, but it must be overcome all the way down the line. The Christian businessman when faced with a moral choice must never ask, "How much will this cost me?" The moment he regards consequences, he dethrones Christ as Lord of his life. His only concern should be with the will of God and the moral quality of the proposed act. To consult anything else is to sin against his own soul.

Again, the pastor when facing his congregation on Sunday morning, dare not think of the effect his sermon may have on his job, his salary or his future relation to the church. Let him but worry about tomorrow and he becomes a hireling and no true shepherd of the sheep. No man is a good preacher who is not willing to lay his future on the line every time he expounds the Word. He must let his job and his reputation ride on each and every sermon or he has no right to think that he stands in the prophetic tradition.

And the same principle is binding upon the religious writer and editor. The scribe who will trim his copy to hold his job is unworthy of public confidence. The editor who will reject an article or a paragraph of an article because he is afraid to accept it is standing in the shadow of the fear of consequences. The publisher who allows desire for profit or the fear of losing sales to decide what books he shall print is on a moral level not too far above the money-changers Christ drove out of the Temple. All these examples point up to a grave modern evil, permitting temporal consequences to decide eternal issues.

A word of caution should be added. Sometimes an act, though good in itself, may, in a given set of circumstances, be better held in abeyance. Only be sure the reason for waiting is the desire to promote the glory of God and bless mankind. Sometimes a word, though true, would be out of season and injurious to someone. Better be silent than to speak a harmful word. Only let the reason for silence be love and not fear.

To sum up: no act, however noble it may seem to be, done from fear of consequences can be good in itself. A good deed done for earthly gain is an evil deed at bottom. Motive imparts moral quality, and without a holy motive there cannot be a holy act.

# It Is Essential That We Think Like God

When we think about spiritual things there is always danger that we think like men instead of like God.

Theological truth cannot enter the mind as a separate substance or as an experience complete in itself. It must be grasped by the mind in an act of response; and the response is conditioned by everything that has gone before in the learner's life. Whether or not we are conscious of doing so, we invariably add something to the truth as it enters (or take something away) to make it fit into the total body of ideas we hold and call "truth."

To show how this works let us imagine two men reading the same passage of Scripture, one a Calvinist who has been brought up on Calvinistic theology from his youth, the other

reared in the Arminian tradition and thoroughly indoctrinated in Arminianism. The passage
they read is Hebrews 6:4–6, "It is impossible for
those who have once been enlightened . . . if
they fall away, to be brought back to repentance." The impressions the Calvinist receives
from these words will differ radically from
those received by the Arminian, yet neither one
will be conscious of adding to, subtracting
from or otherwise altering the passage in any
way. Each will understand the words to mean
exactly what he has been taught that they
mean. The meaning he sees there will appear to
him so natural, so logical and right that he will
wonder how anyone can see any other. (And
sadly enough each will more than likely think
the other a hypocrite who receives his teaching
from the devil. But that is not pertinent to this
particular argument.)

That we must often receive new truth into
minds already cluttered up with old truths,
half-truths and scraps of downright error, and
fit it into the total in such a way that it will appear right and "feel" right to the heart, makes it
extremely difficult for us to grow in grace and
in the knowledge of our Lord Jesus Christ. The
camel may squeeze through the eye of the
needle and be well on his way before some of
us can rid ourselves of our hindrances and get
our minds clear for the free reception of God's
unadulterated truth.

Lest the bare statement of the facts tend to discourage someone, let us look at the other side of the question. Undoubtedly God knows our frame and remembers that we are dust. We should not berate ourselves too much for this weakness. Even an apostle had to have a vision from heaven to free him from some of his old misconceptions and open his heart to a new order of truth (Acts 10:9–16). And we should remember that it does not take a perfect understanding of all truth to save a man and bring him into communion with God. Furthermore, God has sent us a Teacher in the person of the Holy Spirit (John 16:12–15). If we humble ourselves and come to God as little children, He will reveal His Son in us and favor us with revelations of spiritual truth unknown to the wise and the prudent (Matthew 11:25–27).

While it is true that theological truth is modified by its passage through the individual mind, it is also true that there is an anointing which teaches us about all things (1 John 2:27). It is the Holy Spirit, poured out into our hearts (Romans 5:5). There is no danger that we go seriously astray from the truth if we walk humbly, trust completely, search the Scriptures daily, expect divine illumination and lean not on our own understanding. Most assuredly the Holy Spirit will take control of our minds and help us to think like God. Then will be fulfilled the Scripture which says, "But we have the mind of Christ" (1 Corinthians 2:16).

# The New Birth Is a Mystery

I once wrote of the need of the inner witness and pointed out that the lack of it is producing a strain of feeble Christians, weak, half-hearted and pitifully unsure of themselves.

A reader wrote to say in effect that she agreed with me fully and wanted very much to experience the inner witness but did not know how to proceed. She ended her letter with the request that I write something that would make the whole thing clear to her and others.

Much as I should like to comply with this request I am, of course, unable to do so. Indeed the very notion that the things of God can be reduced to a formula is back of many of our spiritual failures. Christian workers, in their eager desire to get the seeker "through," will, it seems, stop at nothing. They try to induce faith by baiting the seeker with Bible texts, all the while smiling and "helping" by voice and gesture. The whole performance, while undoubtedly well-intentioned, acts as a powerful suggestion to raise expectation and predispose the seeker's mind to accept whatever the worker desires that it should. Then follows a series of questions and answers, the questions carefully put in such a way as to suggest the answers, ending usually with the familiar "Well, if He doesn't cast you out, what does He do?" Of course there is only one answer to that question and the bewildered seeker gives it, "Why, He takes me in." This brings on a burst of Amens, along with a deal of backslapping and handshaking, and another convert has been made. That such a convert lacks inward assurance is not surprising.

About the intimate workings of the Holy Spirit in the human heart there is a highly personal relationship in which no third person can share. The sacred work of redemption was wrought in darkness. No strange eye could see what was taking place when the sins of the world entered the holy soul of Christ that He might die under their weight and thus make "his life a guilt offering" (Isaiah 53:10; 2 Corinthians 5:21; Matthew 27:46).

That there is a deep mystery about the new birth is plainly stated by our Lord.

"The wind blows wherever it pleases. You

> hear its sound, but you cannot tell where it
> comes from or where it is going. So it is
> with everyone born of the Spirit."
>
> "How can this be?" Nicodemus asked.
>
> "You are Israel's teacher," said Jesus,
> "and do you not understand these things?
> I tell you the truth, we speak of what we
> know, and we testify to what we have
> seen, but still you people do not accept our
> testimony. I have spoken to you of earthly
> things and you do not believe; how then
> will you believe if I speak of heavenly
> things?" (John 3:8–12)

It is bordering on the irreverent to suggest
that this sovereign work of the Spirit can be in-
duced at the will of a personal worker by
means of a textual recipe. The moment this is
attempted, the Spirit withholds His illumination and leaves the worker and the seeker to
their own designs. And the tragic consequences
are all about us.

All any Christian worker can do is to point
the inquirer to "the Lamb of God who takes
away the sin of the world" (1:29). That was all
John the Baptist did. He did not attempt to create faith in any of his hearers. The Spirit alone
can open the heart, as John well knew. It is our
task to arrest the sinner's attention, give him
the message of the cross, urge him to receive it
and meet its conditions. After that the seeker is
on his own. The individual is out of the hands

of the instructors and helpers and in the hands
of the God with whom he has to do.

It is fear of falling into the hands of God that
makes us so eager to get things reduced to a
formula. We feel that if we can learn the
"secret" of salvation or the "steps" into the
blessed life, we can control our future and
(though we would not admit it) control God
Himself to a large degree. This saves face and
preserves our self-confidence, but it also mutes
the voice of power in the gospel and weakens
the operations of God in the soul. Only the
despairing heart can know the inward witness.

In the final analysis, no one can lead another
to God. All he can do is to lead the inquirer to
the door of the kingdom and urge him onward.
Between God and the returning soul there is a
zone of obscurity through which he cannot see.
It is the light that no man can approach unto
and past which no one can go on his feet or by
means of reason or theological knowledge.
There faith must make its leap of pure trust
into the arms of God crying with Job, "Though
he slay me, yet will I hope in him" (Job 13:15),
or with Newton, "O Lord, I trust in Thee completely, and if I go to hell I'll go down standing
on Thy Word."

It is this utter desperation that brings the witness, and yet I cannot tell anyone how to reach
such a state. All I can do is to urge everyone to
repent and believe on Jesus Christ. If the repentance is genuine and the faith real, all human

confidence will come crashing down and the humbled soul will be forced to make its leap of faith alone.

The reader that cannot find his way from here is in all probability still impenitent. And let him beware of seeking cheap comfort from a text jockey who will cry " 'Peace, peace,' . . . when there is no peace" (Jeremiah 6:14). He had better by far take his Bible and retire to the secret place to seek God alone. If there's hope for him, he'll find it there. But he'll find it nowhere else.

---

# Christian—Or Only a Student of Christianity?

The genuine philosopher, Epictetus, used to say, was not one who had read Chrysippus and Diogenes and so could discourse learnedly on the teachings of these men, but one who had put their teachings into practice. Nothing else would satisfy him. He refused to call any man a philosopher who showed evidence of pride, covetousness, self-love or worldly ambition.

Epictetus was not impressed by eloquence or learning. It was a waste of time for the student to recite the list of books he had read. "What has your reading *done* for you?" he asked his students, and looked not to their words but to their lives for the answer. He required of the young men who sought him out that they bring their lives into immediate harmony with the Stoic doctrines. "If you don't intend to live like a philosopher, don't come back," he told them bluntly. He drew a sharp distinction between a philosopher in fact and a student of philosophy, and would have nothing to do with the mere student. With him it was all or nothing. There was no middle ground.

This is not to advocate the teachings of the Stoics, but to assert that many of "the heathen in their blindness" appear to have more light than some Christians and that the children of this world often show more real wisdom than some of the children of God. For the snare Epictetus warned against is the very one into which multitudes of professed Christians are falling, viz., mistaking the word for the deed and falsely assuming that if they know the teaching of the Christian faith they are therefore in that faith.

The One who said, "Go to the ant, you sluggard;/ consider its ways, and be wise" (Proverbs 6:6), would hardly be displeased if we were to humble ourselves to learn an important lesson from an old Greek philosopher.

It will help us to locate ourselves spiritually if we face up to the rather ungracious question: "Are you a Christian in fact or merely a student of Christianity?" A lot will depend upon the answer, and if ever we should be frank, it is when we examine ourselves to see if we be in the faith. Multitudes tread a hazy path to death because they will not bring themselves under the searching eye of God. They prefer to assume everything is all right, though so to assume is always dangerous and may be deadly.

No one has any right to believe that he is indeed a Christian unless he is humbly seeking to obey the teachings of the One whom he calls Lord. Christ once asked a question (Luke 6:46) that can have no satisfying answer, "Why do you call me, 'Lord, Lord,' and do not do what I say?"

Right here we do well to anticipate and reply to an objection that will likely arise in the minds of some readers. It goes like this: "We are saved by accepting Christ, not by keeping His commandments. Christ kept the law for us, died for us and rose again for our justification, and so delivered us from all necessity to keep commandments. Is it not possible, then, to become a Christian by simple faith altogether apart from obedience?"

Many honest persons argue in this way, but their honesty cannot save their argument from being erroneous. Theirs is the teaching that has in the last 50 years emasculated the evangelical message and lowered the moral standards of the Church until they are almost indistinguishable from those of the world. It results from a misunderstanding of grace and a narrow and one-sided view of the gospel, and its power to mislead lies in the element of truth in contains. *It is arrived at by laying correct premises and then drawing false conclusions from them.*

The truth is that faith and obedience are two sides of the same coin and are always found together in the Scriptures. As well try to pry apart the two sides of a half-dollar as to separate obedience from faith. The two sides, while they remain together and are taken as one, represent good sound currency and constitute legal tender everywhere in the United States. Separate them and they are valueless. Insistence upon honoring but one side of the faith-obedience coin has wrought frightful harm in religious circles. Faith has been made everything and obedience nothing. The result among religious persons is moral weakness, spiritual blindness and a slow but constant drift away from New Testament Christianity.

Our Lord made it very plain that spiritual truth cannot be understood until the heart has made a full committal to it. "If anyone chooses to do God's will, he will find out whether my teaching comes from God or whether I speak on my own" (John 7:17). The *willing* and the *doing* (or at least the willingness to do) come before the *knowing*. Truth is a strict master and demands obedience before it will unveil its riches to the seeking soul.

For those who want chapter and verse here are a few, and there are plenty more: Matthew 7:21; John 14:21; First John 2:4, 3:24, 5:2; First Peter 1:2; James 2:14–26; Romans 1:5; and Acts 5:32.

To sum it up, saving faith is impossible without willing obedience. To try to have one without the other is to be not a Christian, but a student of Christianity merely.

# A Word About
# Superstition

Superstition is inherent in fallen human nature and I suppose there is no one entirely free from it.

There are two classes of men who appear to have come the nearest to getting deliverance from the bondage of superstition: the scientist who has developed a mentality that accepts nothing that cannot be proved and the philosophical skeptic who has taught himself to discount the supernatural. By denying the existence of the spiritual they reduce their hopes and fears to the ordered operation of the natural, but that seems too high a price to pay for their freedom.

With the same broom they use to sweep out banshees, wraiths and apparitions, they also sweep away angels, heaven and (may we reverently say) God Himself. Along with these go belief in prayer, fear of retribution and hope for a future life. Which all is a very unscientific and extremely irrational way to proceed, if you ask me, and especially significant since the very ones who take that way boast above everything else of their scientific minds and their rationality. The man who, in order to get rid of the fear of black cats, must also rid himself of the fear of God is a victim of his own ignorance as surely as the man who nails a horseshoe over his door to bring good luck or carries a horse chestnut in his pocket to ward off an attack of the miseries. Neither man is acting rationally.

Superstition is a child of credulity and thrives on a diet of half-truths and error. It sneaks into the assembly of the saints as did the man without the wedding garment, and unless there is someone present with the gift of discernment, it manages to pass as a true child of faith. But superstition and faith are alike only as a mushroom and a toadstool are alike; one is good nutritious food and the other contains a dangerous poison.

Faith honors God by accepting the biblical revelation of the divine character. Faith lets God be what He says He is and adjusts its concepts accordingly. Superstition degrades the reputation of God by believing things unworthy of Him. One rests upon fact and the other upon fancy.

As I said before, there is probably a streak of superstition in everyone, even in the genuine Christian. Any notions we may have of God that have not been corrected and purified by the Word and the Spirit are likely to have some element of error in them, and the religious beliefs resulting from them will of necessity contain a certain amount of superstition. The Christian who flares indignant at such a statement as this and denies that it describes him is not therefore free from superstition; he merely compounds his faults by adding bigotry and anger to the rest.

But if superstition dishonors God, is it not an evil thing and is not the Christian who harbors it guilty of serious sin against the Majesty in the heavens? The answer to these questions is not as pat as we could desire it to be. An unqualified *yes* or *no* would both be wrong. Here is the reason:

When we first come to God through Christ, we are pagans at heart and our ideas of God are likely to be a mixture of truth, half-truth, ignorance and error. Conversion lifts the veil of darkness in some measure from our minds and allows the light to shine in, but no one who is capable of self-analysis will deny that there still remains a great many shadowy images that have not yet come into clear focus. The newborn child knows God in the deeply spiritual meaning of the word *know* as found in John 17:3, "Now this is eternal life: that they may know you, the only true God, and Jesus Christ, whom you have sent." But this intimate, vital knowledge does not immediately result in a perfect *conception* of God. The mind may yet suffer from imperfect religious teaching, prejudices, mistaken judgments and faulty theological instruction; and in the exact measure that these things are present there will be unworthy and superstitious notions of God and spiritual things.

This kind of error is inevitable at first encounter with God. Let the Christian "follow on to know the LORD" (Hosea 6:3, KJV) and the margin of error will become narrower day by day and year by year as the body of truth becomes greater. So at any given moment in the Christian's life, he may be entertaining imperfect or even unworthy ideas of the Deity, but the Spirit "working unseen like a miner in the depths of the earth" is laboring to purge away the error and fill the heart with pure and lofty notions of the Triune God. While this is going on the patient heavenly Father bears with our imperfection, "for he knows how we are formed,/ he remembers that we are dust" (Psalm 103:14).

# CHAPTER
## 37

# More About
# Superstition

As I said in the previous chapter, at the root of all superstition is an inaccurate and unworthy conception of the character of God.

Character determines expectation. We manage to predict with reasonable exactness the actions of our friends in any given situation because we know what kind of persons they are. It is so with our ideas of God. Our notions of how God will act follow very closely our estimate of His character. God once complained through the psalmist, "You thought I was altogether like you" (Psalm 50:21). Superstition springs out of confusing God's character with man's, a kind of reversal of the original act of God in making man in His own image. Fallen men believe that God is very much like themselves and expect Him to act accordingly.

To be more explicit, men believe God to be whimsical, and consequently expect Him to be impulsive and unpredictable in His dealings with mankind. Out of this notion comes a score of superstitious fancies that have gotten themselves accepted through the years. Various fears originate here. Fear of black cats, omens, signs and magic numbers results from the ignoble idea that God is a kind of playful Puck who delights in practical jokes and Halloween tricks. The only defense against this is to know some word or sign that will protect the victim from the celestial prankster, hence the thousand and one marriage customs, funeral usages, and practices touching birth, death, travel, food, clothing, sleep, planting, harvesting, illness and almost every other phase of our life on earth.

But someone may say, it is not God people fear, but demons—the devil himself and evil spirits generally. The answer is that the whole business is still superstition, for it makes God a party to all this supernatural carryings-on, and even if He is on our side He is unable to help us without certain magic passes on our part, such as knocking on wood, throwing salt over our shoulder or making the sign of the cross. God is therefore subject in some measure to these evil powers and helpless against them unless we play along with the cruel game by staying off the 13th floor of hotels, looking at the new moon over our right shoulder, wearing a charm that has been blessed by a priest or reciting a religious phrase that is supposed to have some special power to terrify the devil. This is all unworthy of God and altogether beneath the dignity of the Majesty in the heavens.

Some persons also think of God as being vindictive, churlish and quick to take vengeance on anyone who is careless about words or gestures or customs, no matter how innocent he may be or how unintentional his error. Of course this is simply a case of judging God by ourselves and thinking that He is altogether such a one as we are. How utterly grateful we should be that when we sinned and fell away from grace in the beginning, God did not act like us. Our eternal hope lies in the fact that at that tragic hour God acted like Himself. His conduct sprang out of His own holy nature and led Him to send His only begotten Son to die for the very ones who had been guilty of such an awful affront to His Person. For this the redeemed shall sing forever, "Worthy is the Lamb, who was slain" (Revelation 5:12).

The cure for superstition is an increased appreciation of the being of God: not names only, but character and being. The idea that the devil is afraid of a word or a gesture is pure superstition. He is not afraid of any name, not even the name Jesus. There are thousands of little boys in Latin America who bear that name, and surely Satan does not stand in fear of them. No, it is not a combination of letters that strikes terror to the heart of Satan. It is the glorious Person who bears the name Jesus whom he fears. To the name Jesus God has added the titles "Lord and Christ," and this means that all power has been given unto Him in heaven and in earth. Back of the name is the sovereign Person of God's Son, our Savior. From this Person Satan flees, but it is a waste of time and effort to try to impress him with mere words and phrases.

In the degree that we know God Himself, we shall be free from superstitious fears; and in the degree that we are affected by signs, gestures, phrases and "religious objects" (as they are naively called), we are in the bonds and snares of superstition.

I have noticed lately among so-called evangelicals a renewed interest in the religious gadgets that our Protestant fathers once threw away to make room for the Holy Spirit. It is becoming more common now to see in our churches (and in some Alliance churches, I regret to say) huge pictures of Christ, crosses on the altar, candles and other symbolic objects. This is the sure way back to formalism and death. In proportion as the Presence of Christ is felt in a congregation these things will be unnecessary, even offensive. And as the Presence lifts and withdraws, these symbols are brought in as poor substitutes.

The human heart must have something to love and fear. If it misses the true God it will make a god of its own. A crowd of persons who pray to a false god is not a church in any sense of the word, even if the word "Christian" or "church" appears on the front of the building.

# Thankful? Yes, But
# to Whom?

There is probably no such thing as a wholly thankless heart. Everyone at some time feels a sense of gratitude for benefits received. This seems to be instinctive, or if not instinctive then surely acquired at a very early age.

That a great many persons fail in the degree of their thankfulness we all know too well. Hardly anyone but has known remorse for his failure to express proper gratitude to father or mother or friend till it was too late. And most of us have felt the chill that comes to those who do acts of kindness for persons who receive them as matters of course without so much as a word of thanks. Even Christ appears to have suffered from such treatment, for after He had healed 10 lepers and only one returned to give Him thanks, He asked rather sadly, "Where are the other nine?" (Luke 17:17). We dare not read too much into this, but it seems fair to assume that He wanted the cleansed lepers to thank Him, and was disappointed when they did not. But even here we must not conclude that these men were wholly thankless. They may quite easily have been grateful to friends and relatives, or even to total strangers who might have helped them in the past, and still have failed to express their thanks to the One who deserved it most.

This habit of thanking everyone but God is not confined to those nine lepers. Enter a plane, a train, a restaurant or any other place where modern civilized men and women meet and mingle and you will see evidences of the same spirit. You will hear thanks given and acknowledged right and left without so much as a mention of God. Somewhere I read of the Christian farm boy who went to college and who in the dining room always bowed his head to thank God before beginning to eat. When some of his fellow students ribbed him for it, he grinned and said, "Hogs don't thank anybody either when they eat their swill." It might have been a bit direct, but I am sure everyone got the point.

It is important that we trace our benefits back to their source and express our thanks to the One "from whom all blessings flow," rather than merely to feel a vague stirring of gratefulness that results in nothing real. I once lived with a fine old couple, neither of whom was a Christian, and I was impressed with the profound sense of gratitude they felt for everything they possessed. When the winter winds moaned through the trees and made the old house tremble, the old man would smile and say, "Ah! How good it is to have a warm place to sleep on a night like this." And the mother would often speak of her large family, now grown and scattered: "How grateful I am that they are all healthy and all mentally sound. I am so thankful." Their gratitude was genuine. Of that there could be no trace of a doubt, but I often wondered who was the recipient of it. Whom were they thanking? They never said.

The irreligious world has its own way of reacting. When things "break" fortunately for a businessman, an athlete or a politician he will slap his hands together and shout, "Great! Wonderful!" He is thanking someone; but whom?

It could be that the old couple of whom I speak were actually meaning to express their thankfulness to God, and that the modern man who shouts his pleasure at his lot in life secretly feels his indebtedness to God; the trouble is that they were and are ashamed to direct their gratitude pointedly to One with whom they are not acquainted. They flee like Adam and hide among the trees of the garden rather than face up to the God they know they have offended. Fear of being thought queer sometimes leads people to express religious ideas in generalities instead of in concrete terms.

It is much easier to say "I am thankful" than to say as Paul did, "Thanks be to God—through Jesus Christ our Lord!" (Romans 7:25). The first does not commit the man. It is broad enough to afford footroom to retreat if someone should challenge him. The second burns its bridges and takes up its cross.

In these last bright brown days of autumn, we will be reminded a hundred times that we have a world of blessings for which we should render thanks. Let's not withhold our expressions of gratitude. Thankfulness that is put into words has a healing effect upon the soul and has a good effect upon those who hear. But let's avoid pagan ambiguity. "For us there is but one God, the Father, from whom all things came and for whom we live; and there is but one Lord, Jesus Christ, through whom all things came and through whom we live" (1 Corinthians 8:6).

# CHAPTER 39

# Not Peace, But a
# Sword

I t should always be kept in mind that the
Church is a divine family and that its loyalties sometimes cut sharply across the ties that
bind earthly families together.

The cross is a sword and often separates
friends and divides households. The idea that
Christ always brings peace and patches up dif-
ferences is found nowhere in His own teachings. Quite the contrary is true. For a man to
cast in his lot with Christ often means that he
will be opposed by his blood relatives and will
find his true family ties only in the community
of regenerated souls.

Surely it is a most desirable thing to be reared
in a Christian home. When a young man or
woman is thus happily situated, conversion to
Christ brings no rift to the family circle but

rather seals and cements the earthly ties. We see sometimes whole families from the aged grandparents to the youngest child all joyously serving the Lord, and hardly anything under the sun could be more delightful. But it is not often so. More often the presence of a true Christian in the home, if it does not actually divide, does at least bring a serious divergence of interest and puts a real strain upon the solidarity of the household.

The weakness of much that passes for the Christian faith these days is seen in the readiness of many professed followers of Christ to make any concessions in order to "get along with people," especially with relatives and in-laws. The philosophy of mid-20th century Christianity is a philosophy of appeasement. Peace and unity have become the Castor and Pollux of the majority of religious leaders, and truth is regularly sacrificed on their altars. The notion that "peace on earth" as the New Testament uses the words, means concord between light and darkness is foreign to the whole traditional Christian position. Our Lord cared nothing for the good will of bad men, nor would He alter one word of His message to stay in favor with anyone, be he Jew or pagan or even a member of His own earthly family. "For even his own brothers did not believe in him" (John 7:5).

No one has understood the meaning of the cross who puts blood ties alongside the ties of the Spirit. "Flesh gives birth to flesh, but the Spirit gives birth to spirit" (John 3:6). All fleshly relationships will be dissolved in the glory of the resurrection, including the relationship between husband and wife. For this reason our Lord said plainly that for some people it would be necessary to break family ties if they would follow Him. "Do you think I came to bring peace on earth? No, I tell you, but division. From now on there will be five in one family divided against each other, three against two and two against three. They will be divided, father against son and son against father, mother against daughter and daughter against mother, mother-in-law against daughter-in-law and daughter-in-law against mother-in-law" (Luke 12:51–53). "If anyone comes to me and does not hate his father and mother, his wife and children, his brothers and sisters—yes, even his own life—he cannot be my disciple. And anyone who does not carry his cross and follow me cannot be my disciple" (14:26–27).

What Christ is saying here is that faith in Him immediately introduces another and a higher loyalty into the life. He demands and must have first place. For the true disciple it is Christ before family, Christ before country, Christ before life itself. The flesh must always be sacrificed to the spirit and the heavenly placed ahead of the earthly, and that at any cost. When we take up the cross, we become expendable, along with all natural friendships and all previous loyalties, and Christ becomes all in all.

In these days of sweet and easy Christianity, it requires inward illumination to see this truth and real faith to accept it. We had better pray for both before time runs out on us.

# chapter 40

# Root out of a
# Dry Ground

One of the most beautiful descriptions of our Savior to be found anywhere is that given by Isaiah in the 53rd chapter of his prophecy: "He grew up before him like a tender shoot,/ and like a root out of dry ground" (verse 2).

Those who have at any time been close to the soil will see at once a young shoot just pushing through the ground and will feel the exquisite precision of the word "tender" when applied to it. The delicate sprout appears to be mostly water, held together one scarcely knows how, and so brittle that it will snap asunder at the slightest touch. Only after the passing of several days does it toughen up enough to endure external pressure without damage.

While a newborn babe is not as fragile as the

tender plant just emerged from the soil, the likeness is too plain to miss, and the prophet spoke well when he compared the one to the other. The helpless, crying human thing is vulnerable from a thousand directions and is wholly dependent for its very life upon parents, neighbors and friends. No one can pick up a day-old baby and not sense the pathetic frailty of it—a barely conscious blob of sweet, perishable life only now arrived from the ancient void of nonexistence.

So our Lord came to the manger in Bethlehem that first Christmas morning, not out of nonexistence, but from eternal pre-existence; not as a son of man only but as Son of Man and Son of God in the fullest sense of both terms; a tender plant and "a root out of a dry ground."

It is quite in keeping with the ways of God that He should make the hope of the world to hang upon something as weak as a new baby. A slip of the hand could have ended the newborn life. All around the Bethlehem manger flowed dark, destructive forces urged on by that ancient and unbelievably cruel dragon called the devil and Satan. All were in black conspiracy to destroy the tender Man-child before He could offer Himself on an altar for the redemption of the world. From the natural viewpoint nothing could have been easier than to kill the Babe before He had learned to say "Father" or "Mother." No bodyguard had He, and the very soldiers that should have protected Him were sent to murder Him. The quiet and harmless Joseph could not save Him from the cold ferocity of the dragon, nor could the sweet young mother afford Him shelter from the destructive power of an iron empire. Yet He lay in complete security, safer in His frailty than if He had been surrounded by an army of a million men; safer than if He had been another Samson, able to slay at one blow a thousand Philistines.

The prophet, with anointed foresight, saw our Lord as He was after He had emerged into human nature and called Him a tender plant; but he saw also His human origin, and this appeared to him, or at least appears to us, more wonderful still: "a root out of a dry ground."

Now everyone knows that moisture is necessary to the germination of seeds, to the swelling of buds and to the sprouting of the root buried there in the ground. Where there is no water, life lies suspended in sleepy inaction. Even the desert plant must have a minimal quantity of moisture before there can be any growth at all. No slip of vegetable life has yet pushed up out of soil that was totally arid. No root has yet sprung out of the dry ground.

Yet Isaiah saw a tender plant grow out of ground where no moisture was; that is, he saw it in prophetic vision, and he knew a miracle was at work. Nature could not have wrought this wonder by herself. The arm of the Lord had done this, and let all the world marvel and be still. As certainly as the dry soil must remain barren, so must apostate Israel be fruitless, so must a virgin maid be childless. No root could grow out of a dry ground.

The prophet had said before that His name should be called Wonderful; and His very first wonder was to be born above nature. We do not wish to read into Isaiah's strangely beautiful words meanings that are not there; but the believing heart that sees the Bible an organic spiritual unit will have no trouble finding here the truth long held sacred by all Christians, the truth of the virgin birth.

Had Israel been like a young woman at the peak of her reproductive powers, the rising of such a prodigy as Jesus from within her might have had some logic in it; but He was born of Israel when her powers had waned and her strength had withered. By no stretch of fancy could anyone who knew Israel in that day have visioned Jesus as her offspring. Israel was dry ground—politically, morally and spiritually effete. Only the few old saints who still remembered the story of Sarah and Isaac could yet hope. And perhaps even they laughed as Sarah had laughed, half in unbelief and half in expectation.

Whatever Christmas may be today, that first Christmas was the celebration of a miracle. A root had come up out of a dry ground.

# Strength from the Indwelling Spirit

Apart from a few brief experiences when the pressure of the world's woes seemed about to crush Him, our Lord while on earth lived a life of relative tranquillity. So at least we would gather from such sketchy biographical material as God has been pleased to furnish us in the four Gospels.

Though Christ was a man of sorrows and though His purity, honesty and penetrating moral insight brought Him into sharp conflict with the hollow religious world around Him, still He maintained a certain quiet poise and freedom from strain throughout His earthly sojourn. Only when He entered purposefully into the dark regions of death to bear the sins of man did He show evidence of exhaustion. But then He was a victim, *the* Victim, and the

normal order of His life was deliberately for-
saken for the tears and blood and dying that
rightfully belonged to those for whom He was
vicariously suffering.

Our Lord was able to work with a minimum
of weariness because He was a man completely
possessed by the Holy Spirit. As a man He did
grow tired and had to sleep and rest to refresh
Himself, but the strain and the exhaustion that
He would otherwise have suffered were spared
Him by the constant quickening of the Holy
Spirit. Peter explained that Christ "went
around doing good and healing all who were
under the power of the devil," *after* God had
"anointed [Him] with the Holy Spirit and
power" (Acts 10:38).

It is possible to work far beyond the normal
strength of the human constitution and yet experience little or no fatigue because the energy
for the work has been provided, not by the
burning up of human tissue, but by the indwelling Spirit of power. This has been realized by a few unusual souls, and the pity is
that they *are* unusual.

Attention has recently been focused upon the
fact that ministers suffer a disproportionately
high number of nervous breakdowns compared with other men. The reasons are many,
and for the most part they reflect credit on the
men of God. Still I wonder if it is all necessary.
I wonder whether we who claim to be sons of
the new creation are not allowing ourselves to

be cheated out of our heritage. Surely it should not be necessary to do spiritual work in the strength of our natural talents. God has provided supernatural energies for supernatural tasks. The attempt to do the work of the Spirit without the Spirit's enabling may explain the propensity to nervous collapse on the part of Christian ministers.

It has been the experience of some great souls that the Spirit actually rests the human organism into which He enters. The Bible would seem to support this belief. Could this be what Isaiah had in mind when he wrote,

> till the Spirit is poured upon us from on
>    high,
>   and the desert becomes a fertile field,
>   and the fertile field seems like a forest.
> Justice will dwell in the desert
>   and righteousness live in the fertile
>     field.
> The fruit of righteousness will be peace;
>   the effect of righteousness will be
>     quietness and confidence forever.
> My people will live in peaceful dwelling
>    places,
>   in secure homes,
>   in undisturbed places of rest.
> Though hail flattens the forest
>   and the city is leveled completely,
> how blessed you will be,
>   sowing your seed by every stream,

and letting your oxen and donkeys range
free. (32:15-20)

Maybe we have been missing something very
wonderful and very necessary. It might be well
if we gave the matter some prayerful attention.
Who knows but we may discover a secret of
health long hidden from the rank and file of
Christians. And God knows we need it.

# CHAPTER 42

# Divine Love Is Neither Blind Nor Dumb

It is unfortunate for the cause of truth that the thinnest skin in the world is that which wraps the saints. God's children are as easily injured as new-hatched hummingbirds, and worst of all, they do not heal readily.

I was reminded of this some time ago when I wrote what was meant to be a good-natured, if realistic, appraisal of a bad book. Not morally bad, understand, but just bad as a book. I was not mad at anybody, and I even tried to soften my review with a bit of what I supposed was recognizable humor.

To the credit of the book's author, he simply ignored me and my review; but a few of my friends were appalled by what I had written. They felt that I had, by my frankness, hurt my

Christian testimony and sinned against the unity of the Spirit and the bond of peace. Had I actually been living the victorious life, they reasoned, I would never have expressed myself so bluntly about a book written by another Christian.

I suppose there will always be sensitive souls who think that the only way to keep sweet is to keep quiet, and who mistake honesty for carnality. These tender-minded saints confuse humility with timidity and believe that credulity and sanctification are synonymous. As they see it, every book written by an evangelical, no matter how sub-standard it may be, should have the wholehearted endorsement of all other evangelicals. Anything less is uncharitable and un-Christian.

One result of this weak attitude is that mediocrity has become normal in the field of evangelical literature. Shoddy thinking and shoddier writing are accepted as earmarks of orthodoxy, to the grief of all better minds and to the delight of the enemies of Christ.

As long as it is held to be an evidence of advanced spirituality to approve whatever is written by gospel Christians and a mark of carnality to criticize anything they write, our direction can only continue to be down. If things go on in their present course, we conservatives will soon be living in a world of soft unreality where smiling, timorous brethren walk about praising the Lord and complimenting each other for literary works so atrocious both in content and style that they would not get past the office boy in a first-class publishing house.

It can only be a cause for deep regret that the fear of offending has silenced the voices of so many men of discernment and put Bible Christianity at the mercy of the undiscerning.

Religious music has long ago fallen victim to this weak and twisted philosophy of godliness. Good hymnody has been betrayed and subverted by noisy, uncouth persons who have too long operated under the immunity afforded them by the timidity of the saints. The tragic result is that for one entire generation we have been rearing Christians who are in complete ignorance of the golden treasury of songs and hymns left us by the ages. The tin horn has been substituted for the silver trumpet, and our religious leaders have been afraid to protest.

It is ironic that the modernistic churches which deny the theology of the great hymns nevertheless sing them, and regenerated Christians who believe them are yet not singing them; in their stead are songs without theological content set to music without beauty.

Not our religious literature only and our hymnody have suffered from the notion that love to be true to itself must be silent in the presence of any and every abomination, but almost every phase of our church life has suffered also. Once a Bible and a hymnbook were enough to allow gospel Christians to express their joy in the public assembly, but now it requires tons of gadgets to satisfy the pagan appetites of persons who call themselves Christians.

In the Old Testament it is recorded that after years of bad leadership had brought Judah to her knees, a new king, Hezekiah, came to the throne. Immediately he called the priests and Levites together and said to them,

> "Listen to me, Levites, consecrate yourselves now and consecrate the temple of the LORD, the God of your fathers. Remove all defilement from the sanctuary."
>
> The priests went into the sanctuary of the LORD to purify it. They brought out to the courtyard of the LORD's temple everything unclean that they found in the temple of the LORD. The Levites took it and carried it out to the Kidron Valley. (2 Chronicles 29:5, 16)

It took a week to get rid of the junk, but when they had obeyed God there followed immediately a sunburst of revival; and the good effects lasted nearly 30 years.

I do not wish to draw too close a parallel between conditions under Ahaz and conditions in the churches today, but every enlightened soul can see how we languish for fearless leaders and bold reformers who will dare to pass holy judgment upon the unscriptural goings on that are being substituted for New Testament Christianity in the majority of our churches.

Somewhere there may be a freckle-faced stripling as yet unknown who will hear the call of God and go forth in dauntless love to become a conscience to the churches. Too many prophets of Jehovah these days are hiding in their caves, but somewhere there may be an Elijah. The bloodless softlings will say at first that he is uncharitable and harsh, but when he gets the prophets of Baal on the run they will tag along behind him, trying to look as if they had been on his side all the time.

Well, he can't come a day too soon.

# CHAPTER 43

# What Easter Is About

The celebration of Easter began very early in the Church and has continued without interruption to this day. There is scarcely a church anywhere but will observe the day in some manner, whether it be by simply singing a resurrection hymn or by the performance of the most elaborate rites.

Ignoring the etymological derivation of the word Easter and the controversy that once gathered around the question of the date on which it should be observed, and admitting as we must that to millions the whole thing is little more than a pagan festival, I want to ask and try to answer two questions about Easter.

The first question is, What is Easter all about? and the second, What practical meaning does it have for the plain Christian of today?

The first may be answered briefly or its answer could run into a thousand pages. The real significance of the day stems from an event, a solid historical incident that took place on a certain day in a geographical location that can be identified on any good map of the world. It was first announced by the two men who stood beside the empty tomb and said simply, "He is not here; he has risen" (Matthew 28:6), and was later affirmed in the solemnly beautiful words of one who saw Him after His resurrection:

> But Christ has indeed been raised from the dead, the firstfruits of those who have fallen asleep. For since death came through a man, the resurrection of the dead comes also through a man. For as in Adam all die, so in Christ all will be made alive. But each in his own turn: Christ, the firstfruits; then, when he comes, those who belong to him. (1 Corinthians 15:20–23)

That is what Easter is about. The Man called Jesus is alive after having been publicly put to death by crucifixion. The Roman soldiers nailed Him to the cross and watched Him till the life had gone from Him. Then a responsible company of persons, headed by one Joseph of Arimathea, took the body down from the cross and laid it in a tomb, after which the Roman authorities sealed the tomb and set a watch before it to make sure the body would not be stolen away by zealous but misguided disciples. This last precaution was the brain child of the priests and the Pharisees, and how it backfired on them is known to the ages, for it went far to confirm the fact that the body was completely dead and that it could have gotten out of the tomb only by some miracle.

In spite of the tomb and the watch and the seal, in spite of death itself, the Man who had been laid in the place of death walked out alive after three days. That is the simple historical fact attested by more than 500 trustworthy persons, among them being a man who is said by some scholars to have had one of the mightiest intellects of all time. That man of course was Saul, who later became a disciple of Jesus and was known as Paul the apostle. This is what the church has believed and celebrated throughout the centuries. This is what we celebrate on the 21st day of April, 1957.

Granted that this is all true, what does it or can it mean to us who live so far removed in space from the event and so far away in time? Several thousand miles and nearly two thousand years separate us from that first bright Easter morning. Apart from or in addition to the joy of returning spring and the sweet music and the sense of cheerfulness associated with the day, what practical significance does Easter have for us?

To borrow the words of Paul, "Much in every way!" (Romans 3:2). For one thing, any question about Christ's death was forever cleared away by His resurrection. He "through the Spirit of holiness was declared with power to be the Son of God by his resurrection from the dead" (1:4). Also His place in the intricate web of Old Testament prophecy was fully established when He arose. When He walked with the two discouraged disciples after His resurrection, He chided them for their unbelief and then asked, " 'Did not the Christ have to suffer these things and then enter his glory?' And beginning with Moses and all the Prophets, he explained to them what was said in all the Scriptures concerning himself" (Luke 24:26–27).

Then it should be remembered that He could not save us by the cross alone. He must rise from the dead to give validity to His finished work. A dead Christ would be as helpless as the ones He tried to save. He "was raised to life for our justification" (Romans 4:25), said Paul, and in so saying declared that our hope of righteousness depended upon our Lord's ability to beat death and rise beyond its power.

It is of great practical importance to us to know that *the Christ who lived again still lives*. "Therefore let all Israel be assured of this: God has made this Jesus, whom you crucified, both Lord and Christ" (Acts 2:36), said Peter on the day of Pentecost; and this accorded with our Lord's own words, "All authority in heaven and on earth has been given to me" (Matthew 28:18), and with the words of Hebrews, "The point of what we are saying is this: We do have such a high priest, who sat down at the right hand of the throne of the Majesty in heaven" (8:1).

Not only does He still live, but *He can never die again*. "For we know that since Christ was raised from the dead, he cannot die again; death no longer has mastery over him" (Romans 6:9).

Finally, all that Christ is, all that He has accomplished for us is available to us now if we obey and trust.

> We are more than conquerors, through our
>     Captain's triumph;
> Let us shout the victory as we onward go.